Leader's Guide for

Primary Source Readings in
Catholic Church History

Leader's Guide for

Primary Source Readings in
Catholic Church History

Michael Greene

Saint Mary's Press™

Genuine recycled paper with 10% post-consumer waste.
5102400

The publishing team included Robert Feduccia Jr., development editor; Lorraine Kilmartin, reviewer; Mary Koehler, permissions editor; prepress and manufacturing coordinated by the prepublication and production services departments of Saint Mary's Press.

Printed in the United States of America

Printing: 9 8 7 6 5 4 3 2

Year: 2013 12 11 10 09 08 07 06 05

ISBN 0-88489-874-1

Contents

Introduction 9

1 Initiation into a Community:
The Body of Christ as a Model of the Church 10
A Rite of Passage

2 The Ship of Salvation:
The Church as an Institution 12
The Dream of Saint John Bosco

3 The Descent of the Holy Spirit:
The Church Is Revealed 14
Acts of the Apostles 2:1–42

4 Expanding the Church:
The Gentiles and the Mosaic Law 16
Acts of the Apostles 15:1–31
Saint Paul's Letter to the Galatians 2:1–21

5 From Movement to Institution:
Practices and Guidelines for the Early Church 18
The Didache

6 Executions and Torture: The Treatment
of Christians During Roman Persecution 20
Pliny's Questions to the Emperor Trajan Concerning
Policy Toward Christians
Emperor Trajan's Reply to Pliny's Questions

7 The Blood of the Martyrs:
A Witness to Love for Jesus 22
The Martyrdom of Saints Perpetua and Felicitas

8 New Freedom: The Roman Empire
Offers Toleration to Christians 24
The Edict of Toleration
The Edict of Milan

9 Two Cities: The Earthly and the Heavenly 26
The City of God

10   True God Became True Human:
Statements on Who Jesus Is   28
     Definition of the Faith

11   Missionary Pope: Saint Gregory the Great
Brings the Light of Christ to England   30
     Ecclesiastical History of the English People
     Letter to Abbot Mellitus

12   A Father's Wisdom:
A Guide for Living in a Community   32
     The Prologue to *The Rule of St. Benedict*

13   Saint Boniface: Missionary to the Germans   34
     Letter Advising Saint Boniface on How to Convert the Heathens
     Report to Pope Zacharias on the Foundation of Fulda Abbey

14   Conflicts of Faith:
Tensions Between the East and the West   36
     Encyclical Letter to the Archiepiscopal Sees of the East

15   Pope Against King:
The Battle Over Appointing Bishops   38
     Correspondence Regarding Lay Investiture

16   "We Adore Thee, Lord Jesus Christ":
The Last Words of the Tiny Friar   40
     The Testament of Saint Francis

17   Gentle and Powerful:
The First Woman Doctor of the Church   42
     Letters to Pope Gregory XI

18   Revival of Prayer: A Springtime for Spirituality   44
     The Imitation of Christ

19   The Revolutionary Monk:
The Protestant Reformation Begins   46
     Writings from Martin Luther

20   "What Is Necessary Is a Different Approach":
The Catholic Reformation   48
     The Way of Perfection

21   "Nor Should They Be in Any Way Enslaved": Europeans Encounter the West   50

Inter Caetera

Sublimus Dei

22   People of Esteem: The Work of Missionaries in China   52

Letter to Francesco Pasio, SJ, Vice-Provincial of China and Japan

23   Money, Workers, and Fairness: Catholic Social Teaching Begins   54

Rerum Novarum

24   The Vicar of Christ: The First Vatican Council Defines Papal Authority   56

Pastor Æternus

25   Year in the Life: An Account of Life in the Spanish Colonies   58

Report on the Mission of San Carlos de Monterey

26   Concern for Souls: A Bishop's Anxiety over the Faith of Slaves in Mississippi   60

A Letter to the Society for the Propagation of the Faith

27   More Than a Tabloid: The Power of *The Catholic Worker*   62

The Long Loneliness

28   Traitor to the State, Herald of the Gospel   64

Letters from a Nazi Prison

29   Reading the Signs of the Times: The Church in the Modern World   66

Gaudium et Spes

30   The Light of the World: The Church as the Sacrament of Salvation   68

Lumen Gentium

Appendix A: Chronological Listing of Chapters   70

Appendix B: Topical Index   71

Introduction

Vision

History often paints a two-dimensional picture—a picture that is both long and wide. Students of Church history can see the development of the People of God over time, and they can see the broad expanse of the Church's influence. Although these are important aspects of learning, the picture remains two-dimensional. To bring texture to such study, a third dimension—depth—is needed.

Church history was made not by actors in a play or movie but by passionate people. Sometimes their passions were inspired by the Holy Spirit. Other times, they were not. But this is part and parcel of the Church's activity. The People of God collectively reflects on events, discerns the Holy Spirit's activity, and then moves ahead hoping to follow the Lord more diligently. By adding the depth of humanity to Church history, the student is better able to join with the Church in the task of discerning God's direction.

Primary Source Readings in Catholic Church History is a collection of readings that moves the student beyond the mere events of history. These readings provide a rich, textured painting of the Church's progression as a pilgrim people by revealing the thoughts, the emotions, and the situations of particular pilgrims. In "The Martyrdom of Saints Perpetua and Felicitas," students will read the diary of a third-century saint who sacrificed all for love of Jesus. In "Pope Against King: The Battle Over Appointing Bishops," a conflict between two men is illuminated by the correspondence between a pope and a king. Both passionately believed they were acting on the Lord's behalf. These primary sources add the depth of humanity to history. They give the students a front-row seat to history and invite them into the constant task of learning how to live today.

Structure

Primary Source Readings in Catholic Church History was designed to be used in conjunction with *The Catholic Church: Journey, Wisdom, and Mission,* the student Church history textbook by Saint Mary's Press (Winona, MN: 1994). *The Catholic Church* moves, for the most part, chronologically. However, some chapters are thematic. You might notice that the readings in *Primary Source Readings* also are not always chronological. This structure is due to the thematic nature of some chapters in *Journey, Wisdom, and Mission.*

If you are not using *The Catholic Church,* appendix A in this leader's guide is a chronological listing of the chapters of *Primary Source Readings* to help you present the readings to the students sequentially. Also, if you are interested in taking a more thematic approach to teaching Church history, appendix B is a topical index.

Content

The chapters in this leader's guide are rather straightforward. Each chapter is designed to help the students learn the main points from the primary sources and apply them to their living. This is done through four components:

- an in-class activity
- a homework extension of that activity
- review questions to help with reading comprehension
- in-depth questions to help students synthesize the readings

The review questions and the in-depth questions are handouts for easy use in class or as a homework activity. We hope you and your students become immersed in the readings and enjoy this front-row seat to history.

Initiation into a Community:
The Body of Christ as a Model of the Church

Summary of the Source:
"A Rite of Passage"

Rev. Aidan Kavanagh, OSB, tells the engrossing story of a fictional ten-year-old boy named Euphemius. His years of preparation for Christian initiation brought Euphemius to a decisive moment, a journey from dusk to dawn—and from death to life. On Easter Sunday morning, after a lengthy fast and a nightlong Liturgy of the Word, the catechumens were led from the assembly hall to the vestibule of the baptistery where they were asked to strip naked. With dawn approaching, deacons or deaconesses rubbed each catechumen with oil in preparation for Baptism. Then, one by one, the catechumens descended into the baptistery where a deacon or deaconess fully immersed them three times as the bishop called them to proclaim their faith. After Baptism, costly and fragrant chrism was poured over their heads as the bishop anointed and sealed them with the sign of the cross. Finally, after years of being dismissed from the assembly hall after the Gospel reading, they were united with the entire assembly to partake in the Eucharist. This is historical fiction at its best! Fourth-century Baptisms *were* sensuous and earthy as well as being a powerful witness and challenge to the Christian community.

Classroom Activity

Students will discover and describe the symbols of initiation as they create a collage.

Materials Needed
☐ magazines that contain images of nature, food, babies, sports, and fashion
☐ poster board (one piece for each group)
☐ glue sticks

1. Divide the class into groups of three to five students.

2. Distribute magazines, poster board, and glue sticks to each group.

3. Instruct the students in the following manner:

❖ Find and cut out pictures that contain oil, water, human touch, light and dark, the human body, new life, death, special food, and meals.

❖ Use the selected images to either re-create a scene from the story or artistically interpret the story.
❖ Find words in ads or articles that describe feelings evoked by these images.
❖ Glue these images and words on the poster board in a professional-looking way.

4. After the collages are finished, ask the groups to each explain their collages to the rest of the class.

5. After the presentations, lead a discussion with the entire class about "A Rite of Passage" by asking the following questions:

❖ Why were items relating to the senses an important part of early Christian initiation ceremonies?
❖ Have you ever perceived the presence of God through your senses?
❖ Did this story or this activity have an impact on your thoughts or feelings about the sacraments of initiation?

6. For student review, distribute copies of handout 1, one to each student, at a time of your choosing.

Homework Extension

Assign the following homework activity in these or similar words:

❖ Turn off all of the lights in your bedroom or in a room with few or no windows. Remain in the darkness for a full 5 minutes. At the end of that time, light one candle. Wait for your eyes to adjust, and make note of what you can see. Pay attention to those things you might never have noticed or paid attention to before. Turn the lights back on. Reflect briefly in writing on your experience of darkness and light using the following points as a guide:

• Why do you think darkness and light were powerful symbols for the early Christians?
• What was it like to sit in the dark for that period of time?
• What did you see by candlelight?
• Describe why you think a lit candle endures as a symbol for Jesus.

Initiation into a Community

The Body of Christ as a Model of the Church

Please provide complete answers to the following questions. You may need to record your answers on a separate sheet of paper.

Review Questions

1. In "A Rite of Passage," what did the bishop instruct the catechumens to do as he entered the vestibule of the baptistery?

2. Why were the catechumens instructed to face westward? eastward?

3. Describe the place where the catechumens were baptized.

4. Describe the roles that the bishop, presbyters (priests), deacons, and deaconesses played.

In-Depth Questions

1. Compare and contrast the fourth-century ritual of initiation with a celebration of infant Baptism, first Eucharist, and Confirmation that you have seen. List some of the more notable similarities and differences.

2. Rev. Aidan Kavanagh wrote a story that could be classified as historical fiction. Why do you think he chose a fictional story to describe the rites of initiation?

3. The rites of initiation include imagery of birth and death. Look for and list examples of both. Does it surprise you that birth and death are images used **in church?** Why are birth and death so powerful? What does it have to do with Christian initiation?

4. "A Rite of Passage" describes an early Christian celebration of initiation as a **feast for the senses.** Choose three symbols from the list below and provide your interpretation of them:
- rubbing a person with fragrant oils
- full immersion in water
- laying on of hands
- light and darkness
- nakedness and new white robes
- words about death and new life
- fasting and sharing in a holy meal

The Ship of Salvation: The Church as an Institution

Summary of the Source: "The Dream of Saint John Bosco"

"The Dream of Saint John Bosco" depicts the Church as a flagship with auxiliary ships surrounding it, and the sea around it is portrayed as a hostile world. The ships' command structure is hierarchical: the Pope captains the flagship, while the bishops command the auxiliary ships. The ships are the churches, while the voyagers are the faithful. The two defenders of this flotilla are the Virgin Mary and the Blessed Sacrament. No matter how violent the attacks, no enemy—no matter how formidable—can sink or destroy the ships. If a ship is damaged, it is repaired at once. If a pope is wounded and dies, another immediately replaces him. A clear chain of command guides the flotilla to its destination. This simple and strong image of the Church with its unbroken command provides an example of the hope people feel from the institutional model for the Church.

Classroom Activity

This activity helps the students understand the hierarchical nature of the Church through an examination of other institutions.

1. Ask the students to name three institutions: the government, the school, and a business are examples of institutions. Write the names of the institutions the students suggest across the top of the board, leaving space between each name.

2. Point out that all institutions have a structure of leadership. Then invite the students to describe the structure of leadership for each of the three institutions listed. Write the students' descriptions below the name of each institution.

3. To prompt a discussion among the students, ask the following questions in these or similar words:

❖ Which of these institutions has a hierarchical structure? [Draw a pyramid △ next to each institution that has a hierarchical structure.]

❖ What purpose does each institution serve? [Write the word "Purpose" below each institution, followed by a short statement of the purpose that the class agrees upon.]

❖ Are any of these institutions more collegial in nature? In other words, is power shared more equally in some than in others? [If no collegial institution is represented on the board, ask for an example of one, such as a board of directors or a student council.]

❖ Do you think the Catholic Church could have survived for over two millennia if it did not have an institutional structure? [Invite opposing views and discussion.]

❖ In what ways does the Church also exhibit a collegial structure?

4. Conclude by asking students to name ways they can see the hierarchical structure of the Church as a gift and to identify ways they can more fully participate in the collegial nature of the Church.

5. For student review, distribute copies of handout 2, one to each student, at a time of your choosing.

Homework Extension

Assign the following homework activity in these or similar words:

❖ In your textbook, reread "The Dream of Saint John Bosco." Then read paragraphs 18–21 in chapter 3, "On the Hierarchical Structure of the Church and in Particular on the Episcopate," of *Lumen Gentium* (*Vatican Council II: The Conciliar and PostConciliar Documents* [Collegeville, MN 1984], pp. 369–374). This document is also posted on the Vatican's Web site.

❖ After your reading, prepare a presentation for class that includes the following topics:

• What explanation of the Tradition does the Catholic Church provide for its hierarchical structure?

• How does "The Dream of Saint John Bosco" bring these words from *Lumen Gentium* to life?

• Which description of the hierarchy was most enjoyable to read and why?

The Ship of Salvation

The Church as an Institution

Please provide complete answers to the following questions. You may need to record your answers on a separate sheet of paper.

Review Questions

1. In "The Dream of Saint John Bosco," what is John Bosco's stated purpose in telling the story of his dream?

2. Why are books and pamphlets included as weapons against the Church?

3. Name the command structure of the flagship and the auxiliary ships.

4. What happens when a ship is damaged or a pope falls?

5. How is the relationship between the Church and the world described in the dream?

In-Depth Questions

1. During the last half of the twentieth century, many countries in eastern Europe were Communist, and Christians were not allowed to publicly gather for worship. In such times, do you think it is important to have a strong chain of command in the Church? Explain.

2. John Bosco's dream paints an image of the Church. Respond to these questions: If the role of Christian imagination is to imagine that which is real, does this dream help you understand the reality of the Church better? What are the strengths and the weaknesses of this image of the Church?

3. The dream of John Bosco depicts the Church as having an unbroken chain of command: as soon as one pope dies, another replaces him as captain of the ship. Why is this unbroken chain of command important?

4. If you were writing a similar story of a dream, what would you place on the two columns as the major defenders or protectors of the Church?

The Descent of the Holy Spirit: The Church Is Revealed

Summary of the Source: "Acts of the Apostles 2:1–42"

In Acts 2:1–42, Saint Luke describes the extraordinary event of the Pentecost. Jewish followers of Jesus from throughout the Mediterranean region had gathered for Pentecost, the traditional Jewish celebration of the new harvest and the Sinai covenant. Suddenly they experienced "the rush of a violent wind" (2) and tongues of fire descending upon them. Using language reminiscent of the great Theophany at Mount Sinai (see Exodus 19:16–25), Luke recounts the descent of the Holy Spirit upon the gathered community.

Luke theologically expresses the core meaning of this event through his account of Saint Peter's *kerygmatic* sermon. Saint Peter proclaims that Jesus's death and Resurrection made this gift of the Holy Spirit possible. Through the Holy Spirit, this community of believers becomes, and continues to be, a reality much more profound than the sum of its parts: it is a living, dynamic body that carries with it the power to forgive sins and Christ's offer of salvation to the world. This event has been recognized as the birth of the Church.

Classroom Activity

Students will look at several Old Testament passages that refer to *fire* and *wind* or *breath* to understand more deeply the symbols at Pentecost.

1. Divide the class into groups of three to five students.

2. Ask the students to look up the following references to fire and wind or breath in the Old Testament:

Fire	Wind or Breath
• Exodus 3:1–6	• Genesis 2:4–7
• Exodus 13:20–22	• 2 Samuel 22:10–11
• Isaiah 6:1–6	• Wisdom 7:24–25
• Isaiah 66:15–16	• Isaiah 59:19–20
• Malachi 3:1–3	• Ezekiel 37:1–10

3. Ask the students to read the passages aloud in their groups and assign the following tasks in these or similar words:

❖ After reading the passages, describe what fire and wind or breath symbolizes in each passage.

❖ Refer to Acts 2:1–42. Write a paragraph that expresses your group's opinion on this question: What is Saint Luke trying to tell Christians through the use of the symbols of fire and wind?

4. Allow the groups to share their paragraphs and lead them in a discussion of this question: What do you think a Christian should learn from a better understanding of these symbols?

5. For student review, distribute copies of handout 3, one to each student, at a time of your choosing.

Homework Extension

Assign the following homework activity in these or similar words:

❖ In terms of Church history, the symbols of fire and wind or breath were significant for the birth of the Church. Refer to your time in class and the insights you gained into Saint Luke's use of the symbols of fire and wind or breath. How are fire and wind still present in the Church? Create something artful that demonstrates how these elements are still present in the Church. To help you with this, you might first look at pictures, or recall the event, of your own Baptism or Confirmation. From that review, make a collage, write a poem, or draw a picture, for example.

The Descent of the Holy Spirit

The Church Is Revealed

Please provide complete answers to the following questions. You may need to record your answers on a separate sheet of paper.

Review Questions

1. In Acts 2:1–42, who, according to Saint Luke, gathers for the celebration of Pentecost?

2. What happens that causes outside observers to remark, "They are filled with new wine" (13, NRSV)?

3. Who addresses the people gathered for this occasion, and what is the speaker's central message?

4. After those who heard this speech were "cut to the heart" (37, NRSV), what did Saint Peter instruct them to do?

5. How do they finally respond to the message they hear?

In-Depth Questions

1. What importance might there be in Saint Peter's being the one to address the entire Church gathered at the time of Pentecost? What does Peter's role appear to be?

2. What does Peter mean when he says, "This Jesus God raised up, and of that all of us are witnesses" (32, NRSV)? What is meant by a **Christian witness**? Do you consider yourself a Christian witness? Explain.

3. Why do you think Baptism became the way and the sign by which new members enter the Church? What might be the significance of such visible signs?

4. Jews from all around the Mediterranean were able to understand what the Galilean Jews were saying to them. List four other possible levels of meaning of this Pentecost experience of oneness and understanding of different languages.

5. It has often been said that the greatest scandal of Christianity is the division that exists between different Christian denominations. If there could be a "new Pentecost" to reunite Christian churches, what would that event look like? Using your imagination, write a description of a reunited Christian church.

Expanding the Church: The Gentiles and the Mosaic Law

Summary of the Sources: "Acts of the Apostles 15:1–31" and "Saint Paul's Letter to the Galatians 2:1–21"

These readings detail the urgent need for a decision by the Apostles and the Church elders. A sudden influx of Gentiles into an almost exclusively Jewish-Christian community prompted serious new questions about what is required of a person who converts to Christianity. Certain Jewish-Christians insisted that Gentile converts fully embrace Mosaic Law, including dietary restrictions and male circumcision. Others said that following Jesus fulfilled all the requirements of the Law. In this tension, a vigorous and emotional debate ensued. Eventually the Church came to the consensus that unnecessary burdens should not be placed on these converts. Beyond the immediate issue at hand, a new consensus about the faith, the Law, and the very nature of the Church emerged.

Classroom Activity

In this activity, students discuss a modern-day issue of law and culture that has parallels to those discussed in the New Testament readings.

1. Divide the class into two groups. Tell the groups that they have just become the leaders of the Church, and a worldwide synod at the Vatican has just begun. The issue being discussed today is the following request:

❖ Several Asian communities in the world have requested that they be granted permission to use rice-based wafers for Communion rather than wheat because wheat bread and wheat-based foods are not common in their cultures.

2. Assign each group a position on the issue. Group 1 should be assigned the position that rice cakes should not be allowed. The following statements can be used to shape their position:

• Jesus used unleavened bread as he brought new meaning to the Jewish Passover meal. God instructed the Israelites to use unleavened bread for this meal.

• By extension, the Christian Church has traditionally used unleavened wheat bread.

• It is important for Christians to be united in their practices throughout the world.

Group 2 should be assigned the position that rice cakes should be allowed. The following statements can be used to shape their position:

• The Eucharist would have more meaning to people if a food from their culture is used.

• Even though it is not wheat, it is a grain and is in harmony with the Last Supper.

3. Allow time for the two groups to discuss the central points of their position. Then lead the class in a discussion in which they reach a consensus on whether it is appropriate in certain cultures to use rice cakes rather than bread. Briefly explain that a consensus is a group decision in which all members give full assent for the common good of all.

4. Once the students reach a consensus, ask them to name all the values that went into their decision. Write these values on the board as they are named.

5. For student review, distribute copies of handout 4, one to each student, at a time of your choosing.

Homework Extension

Assign the following homework activity in these or similar words:

❖ Imagine that an ecumenical council (such as Vatican Council II) is about to be called, and the bishop of your diocese has invited all parishioners in the diocese to submit their concerns for the council in the form of proposals to be discussed. What are some of the most important issues you would want to be addressed and why? Write your answers on a sheet of paper to turn in at the next class meeting.

Expanding the Church

The Gentiles and the Mosaic Law

Please provide complete answers to the following questions. You may need to record your answers on a separate sheet of paper.

Review Questions

1. Acts of the Apostles 15:1–31 concerns dissension in the community and debate. What issue is being debated?

2. Where is the debate settled? Who is involved in the discussions?

3. In Galatians 2:1–21, what reason does Saint Paul give for becoming an apostle to the Gentiles?

4. What does Paul disagree with Cephas (Peter) about? Why?

5. Name the key leaders mentioned in the primary sources and explain the significance of each being a part of the Council of Jerusalem.

In-Depth Questions

1. Write or outline a brief description of the Council of Jerusalem and the reasons it was convened.

2. Based on what you can observe from this first council, what seems to be necessary for a Church meeting to be considered a council?

3. What does Paul confront Peter (Cephas) about in Galatians? Why?

4. Why do the Gentile Christians send Paul and Barnabas and several other leaders of the Church to the Apostles and the elders of the Church in Jerusalem? What difference would it have made had those Gentile Christians attempted to resolve this issue within their own community?

5. By what process did the Council of Jerusalem make its final decision? What role does Peter play in the process?

6. Imagine that you are a first-century Christian. What significance do you think the decision made at the Council of Jerusalem will have for the future of the Church? Turning to the present time, upon what contemporary issue would the Council of Jerusalem's decision still have relevance?

7. Relate the events of the Council of Jerusalem to the Church's experience at Pentecost and explain how both relate to this idea: the whole is greater than the sum of its parts.

From Movement to Institution: Practices and Guidelines for the Early Church

Summary of the Source: *The Didache*

The *Didache* demonstrates the need of the early first-century Church to codify beliefs and practices. At a time when the Church was experiencing rapid growth, this document directed Christians in matters of food, sacraments, selection of bishops, and holiness. The *Didache* urges Christians to avoid circumstances or items associated with nonbelief, such as certain foods offered to idols. It provides a practical directive to make sure that Baptism is practiced in such a way that its meaning is clear and visible. The *Didache*, revealing that the Our Father had already become a central prayer for Christians, instructs Christians to pray it frequently. Its directives on the Eucharist provide evidence that this meal had become the central event of Christian communal life. The *Didache* also shows that the "election" of Bishops and deacons by God through the discernment of the local community had become the clear mode of succession of the Apostles. Finally, it instructs believers to be prepared for Christ's Second Coming by meeting frequently with one another and by conforming their lives to the perfection of Christ in both faith and action.

Classroom Activity

Students will examine the *Didache* to discover the pressing issues of the first-century Church and of the modern Church. They will be challenged to discover ways they can have an impact on the current issues they identify.

Materials Needed
☐ newsprint
☐ colored markers

1. Divide the class into seven groups of equal size. Assign each group one of the seven sections of the *Didache*.

2. Instruct the groups in the following manner:

❖ Write the title of the assigned section at the top of the newsprint.
❖ Make two columns.
❖ In the left column, write the words "issue then" and briefly describe the issue this section addresses.
❖ In the right column, write the words "issue now" and briefly describe a similar issue the Church addresses today.
❖ Across the bottom of the newsprint, write the words "pressing issue" and describe an important issue that you think the Church needs to address right now.

3. Each group should present its work to the class. Use the information gathered for a class discussion. Conclude by asking the students how they can help address today's pressing issues.

4. For student review, distribute copies of handout 5, one to each student, at a time of your choosing.

Homework Extension

Assign the following homework activity in these or similar words:

❖ The *Didache* can be thought of as a handbook of practical information for early Christians. Look at your school handbook and examine the topics it covers. How does this handbook help your school community? What are its limitations? Either write your answers to these questions, or be prepared to discuss these questions in class as you are instructed.

From Movement to Institution

Practices and Guidelines for the Early Church

Please provide complete answers to the following questions. You may need to record your answers on a separate sheet of paper.

Review Questions

1. What is the definition of the word **didache**?

2. In the section titled "The Law of Perfection and Foods," what suggests that this document will serve as a practical guide to the beliefs and practices of the Church?

3. What elements are essential for Christian Baptism?

4. Why should Christians fast on days other than Mondays and Thursdays?

5. Who should or shouldn't come and break bread on the Lord's Day?

6. During a Christian's life, while waiting for the last day, what else should he or she be doing?

In-Depth Questions

1. What might some of the reasons have been for giving public instruction on such things as the celebration of Baptism and the Eucharist? Discuss.

2. Which of these practices described in the *Didache*—Baptism and the Eucharist—is part of our Catholic Tradition today? Are any of these completely out of date?

3. The Catholic Church takes the position that only Catholics in good standing with the Church should receive Communion. Does anything in the *Didache* support this view? Where do you stand on this?

4. How often should members of the Christian community celebrate the Eucharist together? Discuss what you think is the importance of attending Mass every Sunday.

Executions and Torture:
The Treatment of Christians During Roman Persecution

Summary of the Sources:
"Pliny's Questions to the Emperor Trajan Concerning Policy Toward Christians" and "Emperor Trajan's Reply to Pliny's Questions"

Two second-century letters—one from the Roman governor Pliny to the emperor Trajan and the second from Trajan in reply to Pliny—elucidate the circumstances under which Christians were sporadically tortured by the Roman Empire in the first three centuries. Pliny is clear in that he had already assumed authority to torture and execute Christians for refusing to renounce their faith and for refusing to worship the image of the emperor and the statues of the Roman gods. The Christians were seen as a threat to the unity in the empire. Pliny's cruel punishment of Christians had an effect. Some Christians willingly renounced their faith. Yet others defied Pliny's edict that demanded Christians deny their faith. Christianity continued making inroads in many towns and villages. In his letter, Pliny appears committed to stay this Christian "superstition." Interestingly, Emperor Trajan discouraged Pliny from deliberately going after the Christians, although he condoned Pliny's actions against them. His rationale was that it would be worse to call too much attention to the Christians' cause. Therefore, if Christians wished to remain Christians, they would do well to remain quiet about their faith.

Classroom Activity

Through a comparison made to the film *Schindler's List* (1993, 197 minutes, rated R), the students will be asked to consider motivations and responses to religious persecution.

1. Obtain a copy of the film *Schindler's List* and have the students view the scene where the Jews are moved into the Warsaw ghetto. (This scene begins about 18 minutes into the film. The scene is approximately 5 minutes long and does not contain disturbing images such as those of the executions found later in

the film. However, please obtain parental permission for students who are minors to view an R-rated movie, and use your best judgment regarding the appropriateness of the excerpt.)

2. Ask the students the following questions to facilitate a discussion:

❖ How was the treatment of Jews in Poland similar to the treatment of Christians in the Roman Empire under Pliny and Trajan?
❖ How are the situations different?
❖ What, do you think, motivates people to such hatred as seen in this movie clip and in these letters?

3. Ask the students to imagine themselves as Roman governors who have heard of Pliny's treatment of the Christians. Instruct them to write a letter to the emperor arguing against the persecution of the Christians. Ask them to submit their letters to you at the end of class.

4. For student review, distribute copies of handout 6, one to each student, at a time of your choosing.

Homework Extension

Assign the following homework activity in these or similar words:

❖ Find an article from a recent newspaper that shows a form of discrimination in the United States. Write a review of this article, discussing the following questions:

• Briefly explain the event or events you read about. Why do you consider this discrimination?
• What is the reason, either implied or given, for the action(s) taken against the discriminated person(s)?
• What do you see as right or wrong about these actions? Why?
• Considering this and other forms of discrimination in the United States, do you see any threat to your own religious freedom?

Executions and Torture

The Treatment of Christians During Roman Persecution

Please provide complete answers to the following questions. You may need to record your answers on a separate sheet of paper.

Review Questions

1. Why did Pliny, a governor of a territory in the Roman Empire, write to Emperor Trajan?

2. What did Pliny tell Trajan about the way he had already dealt with Christians, and why?

3. What major requirement did Pliny place on Christians, and how had they responded?

4. Did Trajan fully agree with Pliny's actions toward Christians? Why?

5. Name three things that can be learned about Christians from these two letters.

In-Depth Questions

1. From the context of these two letters, what does the purpose of religion in the Roman Empire seem to be?

2. Does the sizable number of Christians who left their faith under persecution surprise you? Why? Does it surprise you that many Christians remained committed to their faith?

3. Why, do you think, did Pliny **first** torture and execute Christians and **then later** ask for the Emperor Trajan's opinion about the treatment of Christians?

4. Imagine you are a second-century Christian. How would your faith hold up to the threat of torture and execution?

5. In the male-dominated world of the second century, what significance might there have been that Pliny discussed **deaconesses** in his letter to Trajan?

6. Do you think some people are "persecuted" at your school for standing up for the Gospel?

The Blood of the Martyrs: A Witness to Love for Jesus

Summary of the Source: "The Martyrdom of Saints Perpetua and Felicitas"

Saint Perpetua wrote this startlingly blunt account of the almost unimaginable cruelty she and her companions experienced. Her words are contained within the narrative of another writer who wished to make Perpetua's story known. Perpetua was a catechumen—and a very young wife with a baby. Perpetua and her twenty-two-year-old brother were the only catechumens in their family. While Perpetua was in prison, her father pleaded with her to save her life by renouncing her Christian faith. Perpetua refused. Her father's anger and inability to understand her conviction caused her deep pain. But Perpetua's faith and a mystical vision kept her strong.

While in prison awaiting her martyrdom, she was baptized. Perpetua and her companions—Felicitas, Revocatus, Saturninus, and Secundulus—then faced their deaths together. Their captors brought Perpetua and Felicitas nude into an amphitheater before a crowd of spectators. When even the unruly crowd was horrified by this indignity, Perpetua and Felicitas were taken away. Later they were returned—this time robed—to the arena where a mad heifer struck them down. Perpetua and Felicitas were finally brought to a dais where they gave each other a final kiss of peace and died at the hands of gladiators.

Classroom Activity

This activity focuses on the difficulty of standing up for one's convictions, with parallels made to Saints Perpetua and Felicitas.

1. Ask the students to identify five teachings from the Scriptures or the Church's Tradition that would not be popular today. (The Church's stance on preferential options for those who are poor or on premarital sex are examples.) Write the students' responses on the board.

2. After the five teachings have been named, ask the students to identify what qualities or resources a person needs to take a public stance in favor of these teachings. A conviction that the stance was really true, a group of people who would always love and support the person, or a love for truth are examples. Write the students' responses on the board.

3. Ask the students to review the qualities and resources. After they review the list, they are to rate themselves on a scale of 1 to 5 (with 5 being high and 1 being low) on their possession of the qualities and resources. Ask them to then close their eyes and place their heads on their desks. Then ask the following questions:

❖ Please raise your hand if you give yourself a 1.
❖ Please raise your hand if you give yourself a 2. [Continue in this manner until you reach 5.]

Next to each quality recorded on the board, write down the number of hands that were raised for that quality. Invite the students to open their eyes and look at the responses.

4. Ask the students the following questions:

❖ How, do you think, would Saints Perpetua and Felicitas have responded?
❖ How many of you would like to increase your rating?
❖ How do you think you could increase your rating?

5. Conclude by having the students join in praying the following prayer:

Saints Perpetua and Felicitas, your perfect love for Jesus cast away any fear of death. We ask that you pray for us. When we are tempted to renounce our convictions, may the strength of the Holy Spirit help us stand up for what we know is right. We ask this through Jesus the Lord. Amen.

6. For student review, distribute copies of handout 7, one to each student, at a time of your choosing.

Homework Extension

This assignment will help students identify people who have made difficult choices by standing by their convictions. Assign the following homework activity in these or similar words:

❖ Locate a newspaper or magazine article that describes a difficult moral or spiritual choice a person faced. Write an essay describing the situation and how the person made the choice. If possible, photocopy or print the article and turn it in with your essay. Was faith part of the decision-making process? What difference did, or could, faith make? Finally, how do you think you would have handled a similar situation?

The Blood of the Martyrs

A Witness to Love for Jesus

Please provide complete answers to the following questions. You may need to record your answers on a separate sheet of paper.

Review Questions

1. Why was Perpetua arrested? What did her father want her to do?

2. What reasons did Perpetua give for disobeying the Roman governor?

3. What consequences did Perpetua and Felicitas face for their disobedience?

4. What were the attitudes of Perpetua and her companions toward death?

In-Depth Questions

1. What were some of the feelings you experienced while reading this account of the martyrdom of Saints Perpetua and Felicitas?

2. With an infant and a husband at home, why do you think Perpetua chose martyrdom when she could have saved her life? Would you make the same choice?

3. What was the purpose of making the martyrdom of Christians a public spectacle?

4. At this time, Christianity was still a new religion. Now that Christianity is two thousand years old, is there less urgency for people to witness to their faith by making difficult choices? Please explain.

5. What importance did martyrdom have for the early Church? Would the Church be different today if there had been no martyrs?

6. Under what circumstances might you have to make a difficult and unpopular choice? How might the testimony of Perpetua help you make that choice?

New Freedom: The Roman Empire Offers Toleration to Christians

Summary of the Sources: "The Edict of Toleration" and "The Edict of Milan"

The first reading is the Edict of Toleration (AD 311), promulgated by Emperor Galerius. After criticizing Christians for their lack of good sense and for not supporting the state religion, Galerius decided that Christianity should be tolerated in the empire after all. Galerius thought that rather than worship no god at all, as many had chosen to do, Christians should be permitted to privately pray for the good of the state and for their own health.

Just two years later, Emperor Constantine and Licinius Augustus, the ruler of the Eastern Empire, further expanded toleration by issuing the Edict of Milan. This document presented a united front across the empire that affirmed the value of free public worship. It recognized the right of assembly in public places, the right of ownership of such places, and the value of religion for the prosperity and public order of the state. Constantine ordered that the edict be announced throughout the empire. In a short time, Christianity was no longer a religion of the politically oppressed.

Classroom Activity

This activity and the homework extension explore the relationship between church and state and help students identify the Church's teaching on religious liberty.

1. Divide the class into four groups of equal size. Randomly assign one of the following statements to each group:

❖ The state has the right to regulate which religion(s) may be practiced for the sake of public order.
❖ The Church has a right to require the state to make Christianity the state religion, so long as the majority of the people are Christians.

❖ The state has no ultimate authority over religion; therefore, it must grant all religions the equal right to practice their beliefs, so long as no one is physically, emotionally, or economically hurt.
❖ The Church has an obligation to allow the state to operate as it wishes, even if it means that its right to worship, to teach, and to influence society is greatly diminished.

2. Ask the groups to each prepare a defense for their statement. After the groups briefly present their points of view, ask the students to discuss the issue in hopes of reaching a consensus about which one is most correct.

3. If the students reach a consensus, write their final statement on the board; otherwise, have them name the issues that prevented a consensus.

4. For student review, distribute copies of handout 8, one to each student, at a time of your choosing.

Homework Extension

Through this assignment, the students will discover the Church's teaching on its relationship with other religions. Assign the following homework activity in these or similar words:

❖ Read the "Declaration on Religious Liberty" from the documents of the Second Vatican Council either in print (*Vatican II: The Conciliar and Post Conciliar Documents, New Revised Edition*, Austin Flannery, O.P. editor. [Collegeville, MN: Liturgical Press, 1984], pp. 799–812) or at the Vatican's official Web site. After reading this document, explain in writing the Catholic Church's point of view about the relationship between church and state. Be prepared to discuss your answer when the class meets again.

 New Freedom

The Roman Empire Offers Toleration to Christians

Please provide complete answers to the following questions. You may need to record your answers on a separate sheet of paper.

Review Questions

1. What opinion of Christianity did Emperor Galerius express at the beginning of his Edict of Toleration?

2. What did this edict allow?

3. Why did Galerius make this change in policy toward Christians?

4. What rights did the Edict of Milan add to those granted by the Edict of Toleration?

5. What reason did Constantine give for issuing this edict?

In-Depth Questions

1. In your opinion, would Christianity have grown or would it even have survived if it had continued to be outlawed in the Roman Empire?

2. What effect would the outlawing of Christianity have on you and on your Church community today?

3. Christianity has been declared illegal in modern times in such places as China, Poland, and the former Soviet Union; yet the Church survived. Why do you think it survived as an underground religion?

4. Compare and contrast the motivations of Galerius and Constantine in granting greater tolerance toward Christianity. What would Christians today say about why their religion should be tolerated?

Two Cities: The Earthly and the Heavenly

Summary of the Source:
The City of God

In the first selection of *City of God* (Book XIV, chapter 28), Saint Augustine describes the earthly city and the heavenly city. For Augustine, both realities are good, but only the latter is full and complete. For instance, Augustine describes the earthly city as that which finds enough strength in itself and in its rulers, while the heavenly city finds its ultimate strength in God.

The second selection (Book XV, chapter 4) provides a more elaborate description of the earthly city. Even though this temporal reality is good, it cannot attain complete fulfillment because of its limited nature, and therefore it often finds itself at odds or even at war with itself. Augustine says, for example, that the earthly city makes war to attain peace. But the earthly city fails to understand that the peace attained is not a permanent peace and is sometimes won at a great cost. The only "peace never-ending" is the peace of the heavenly city.

In the third selection (Book XXII, chapter 30), Augustine describes the goal of the heavenly city, a goal that is sometimes referred to as the eighth day of Creation. Augustine presents a vision of ideal relationship, in which each person is fulfilled according to whomever he or she has become in life—in deed, spirit, and intellect. The heavenly city is also an ideal community where all are fully and harmoniously united into the structure of the community.

Classroom Activity

This activity will help students learn about Augustine's *City of God* through their creation of a visual interpretation of the *City of God*.

Materials Needed
- ☐ large pieces of paper or newsprint, one for each group
- ☐ sets of colored markers, one for each group

1. Divide the class into small groups of five or six. Give each group a large piece of paper or newsprint and a set of colored markers.

2. Provide the following instructions in these or similar words:

- ❖ Each group will produce a picture of the *City of God*.
- ❖ First, brainstorm what and who should be included in the city. One member of your group should record the brainstormed ideas on a piece of notebook paper.
- ❖ Prioritize what belongs in the city and where it belongs in the city.
- ❖ On the paper or newsprint, create your group's *City of God* by drawing the people, the places, and the things you brainstormed. Be sure to show their relationships to one another.
- ❖ After you have created your drawing, have one or two members of your group show and describe your group's *City of God* to the class.

3. After the groups have made their presentations, post the drawings around the room and then ask the following question:

- ❖ What does the heavenly city teach us about the way we should live now?

4. For student review, distribute copies of handout 9, one to each student, at a time of your choosing.

Homework Extension

Provide each student with a copy of Book X, chapter 6, of Augustine's *Confessions*. Many editions of *Confessions* are available on the Internet, including the "Church Fathers" page at the New Advent Web site. Tell the students that after they read the selection, they are to write a one-page essay that answers the question, How are the two cities presented by Augustine in *City of God* reflected in Augustine's own personal life and conversion?

Two Cities

The Earthly and the Heavenly

Please provide complete answers to the following questions. You may need to record your answers on a separate sheet of paper.

Review Questions

1. What does Saint Augustine mean by the **earthly city** and the **heavenly city**?

2. According to Augustine, what are some of the ways the heavenly city can be recognized?

3. What are some of the limitations of the earthly city, according to Augustine?

4. What image does Augustine use to describe the city of God and the way each person there will be rewarded?

5. There are seven days in the Creation story in Genesis. What does Augustine mean by the **eighth day?**

In-Depth Questions

1. Augustine's *City of God*, as a whole, is a defense of Christianity. Do you think it is important for Christians to be able to use reason and logic to defend their faith? Why or why not?

2. What have you experienced or studied regarding the Church that resembles Augustine's heavenly city?

3. Briefly explain what Augustine means by the **eight ages**. Do you think human history has certain plateaus that represent new levels of spiritual or intellectual awareness? Give three or four examples.

4. The Church supports the understanding that the beliefs of a Christian politician should influence his or her decisions. Write a profile of a hypothetical politician who would seek the city of God while in office. Would this view make a difference in how a politician approaches health care, education, the right to life, and war?

True God Became True Human: Statements on Who Jesus Is

Summary of the Source: "Definition of the Faith"

This reading demonstrates the development of doctrine from the Council of Nicaea to the Council of Chalcedon in the face of challenges to orthodox belief. One challenge—Arianism—held that Jesus, the Word, was somehow a creation of God and not equal to God. According to this view, Jesus is neither fully human nor fully divine. On the other hand, Nestorianism held that Jesus was essentially a human who was linked to the Word of God by some sort of special favor from God. Simply put, Nestorianism held that Jesus is fully human but not fully divine.

The Council of Nicaea settled the issue of Jesus's divinity by stating in precise, philosophical terms that Jesus—the Son of God—is truly and eternally begotten of God, not created. In other words, God the Father and God the Son are of the same essence and are equal. Later, the Council of Constantinople defined Jesus's humanity, again in clear and precise philosophical language. The council said that Jesus is one in essence with the Father and also that Jesus was born of a woman and is truly human. And, as any human would, Jesus suffered when he was crucified. Only because he is God could he rise from the dead. Therefore, Jesus has only one essence, but two natures: God and human.

Classroom Activity

This activity helps students discover the importance of reaching consensus about an important issue.

1. Propose the following issue: Even though the Catholic Church officially opposes capital punishment, there is wide disagreement among Catholics about this issue.

2. Divide the class into groups of five or six students. Assign the following tasks in these or similar words:

❖ Choose a member of your group to record three statements that define your group's thoughts about (1) the right to life, (2) the purpose of punishment, and (3) the meaning of rehabilitation.

❖ After all the groups have written their statements, each group should pair up with another group. These new groups of ten to twelve students are to each reach consensus definitions on the three topics again. Continue this process of defining, regrouping, and defining again until the entire class has agreed upon statements that define (1) the right to life, (2) the purpose of punishment, and (3) the meaning of rehabilitation.

3. Conclude by asking the following questions:

❖ How does this process resemble the events at Chalcedon?

❖ How obliged are we to follow the beliefs we have defined?

❖ What do you think this process indicates about following the Church's teaching on different matters?

4. For student review, distribute copies of handout 10, one to each student, at a time of your choosing.

Homework Extension

Assign the following homework activity in these or similar words:

❖ A complaint is sometimes raised against cafeteria Catholics, those Catholics who like to pick and choose which aspects of Catholic teaching they want to live by. Write a brief essay reflecting on (a) the critical importance of unity in belief and (b) whether a person can legitimately disagree with Church teaching and still be a Catholic.

True God Became True Human

Statements on Who Jesus Is

Please provide complete answers to the following questions. You may need to record your answers on a separate sheet of paper.

Review Questions

1. What main issue is described as the reason for calling the council at Chalcedon?

2. What level of authority does this council have over the matters discussed, according to this document?

3. What main issue is resolved at the council at Nicaea?

4. What is the difference between **begotten** and **made**, with regard to the second Person of the Trinity?

In-Depth Questions

1. What is the difference between an essential belief and a nonessential belief in matters of faith? Explain.

2. The doctrine of the union of Christ's humanity and divinity is known as the **hypostatic** union. Based on your reading, describe this doctrine in your own words.

3. What problem could exist for Christian faith if Jesus were not fully human? What problem could exist if Jesus were not fully divine?

4. What effect does "The Definition of Faith" have on the faith lives of everyday men and women? What might the consequences have been if such definitions of faith had never been written?

5. The councils that developed the creeds defined right and wrong thinking about Christian faith. How can wrong thinking hurt unity in the Church? Can you think of anything else of significance that can hurt unity among followers of Jesus? Explain.

Missionary Pope:
Saint Gregory the Great Brings the Light of Christ to England

Summary of the Sources: *The Ecclesiastical History of the English People* and the "Letter to Abbot Mellitus"

These selections provide a glimpse into the holiness, the genius, and the concerns of Saint Gregory the Great. Among Gregory's greatest concerns were the qualities needed by those who serve the Church as bishop and pope. The great Church historian, Saint Bede the Venerable, believed that the most important quality is the capacity to lead by example. Bede tells us that Gregory gave money to the poor rather than build elaborate churches with expensive ornamentation. Such action demonstrated Gregory's highest value: the salvation of souls.

Before he was elected pope, Gregory witnessed the beauty and goodness of the English people during an encounter with some slave boys. Gregory, remembering these boys when he became pope, wanted to bring Christianity to England by sending missionaries. In a letter to the missionary Abbott Mellitus, Gregory instructed Mellitus to respect and maintain the English people's existing places of pagan worship so that after their conversion, the new Christians could continue to use their familiar places for worship. This proposal might seem odd today, but Gregory's genius is quite evident. He wished to affirm the good within the English people and their culture and, at the same time, invite them into Christian faith and life.

Classroom Activity

Students discover their own concern for the well-being and the salvation of others.

Materials Needed
☐ newsprint or poster board
☐ markers

1. Divide the class into groups of four or five; distribute one sheet of newsprint or poster board and two or three markers to each group. Provide the following instructions in these or similar words:

❖ Saint Gregory had an encounter with a group of people for whom he felt compassion. Later in life when he was in a position of greater power, he mobilized people and resources to help serve those people from his past.

❖ I ask you to recall a time you felt compassion for someone. Share this experience with your group.

❖ Once everyone in the group has had a chance to share, choose a person or group of people from one of the shared stories of compassion. Your task is to create a display that illustrates a plan to serve this person (or someone like him or her) or group of people.

❖ Your plan should do the following:

  • Identify the problem or the suffering that the individual or group of people faced.

  • Identify what is needed to bring resolution to the problem.

  • Include details on how you would acquire the necessary resources and how you would recruit people to help in the effort.

2. After allowing the groups the time to work on their plans, invite the groups to present their plans to the rest of the class. As a large group, discuss the proposals.

3. Post the illustrated plans around the room and challenge the students to act on their plans.

4. For student review, distribute copies of handout 11, one to each student, at a time of your choosing.

Homework Extension

Use these or similar words to assign the following homework activity, which invites students to more deeply examine the life of Saint Gregory the Great:

❖ Go to an Internet search engine and type in "Saint Gregory the Great." From the listed Web sites, choose one with a biography of Pope Gregory, and then read the biography. When you have finished reading, write a personal reflection about his life. Your reflections should include answers to these questions: What do you most admire about Gregory the Great? What qualities of his would you like to imitate?

Missionary Pope

Saint Gregory the Great Brings the Light of Christ to England

Please provide complete answers to the following questions. You may need to record your answers on a separate sheet of paper.

Review Questions

1. What event prompted Saint Bede to write about Gregory in his *Ecclesiastical History of the English People?*

2. When Gregory wished to go to England as a missionary, what prevented him from doing so?

3. What did Pope Gregory do for the people of England to help their conversion to Christianity?

4. In his letter to Abbot Mellitus, what did Gregory tell Mellitus to do with pagan churches? Why?

In-Depth Questions

1. Several times, Saint Bede mentioned Pope Gregory's frailty and pain. How do you think such suffering might have affected Gregory as pope?

2. The reading recalls Gregory's encounter with some English slaves that moved his heart with compassion. Can you recall a time when you were similarly moved with compassion? Describe your experience.

3. Imagine you are going to interview Gregory. What five questions would you ask him? Why did you choose those questions?

A Father's Wisdom: A Guide for Living in a Community

Summary of the Source: "The Prologue to *The Rule of St. Benedict*"

The Rule of St. Benedict contains a marvelous paradigm for Christian living. Although the *Rule* was written as a guide for monks, it has profoundly influenced lay Christians as well. The prologue sets forth a vision for Christian community. According to Benedict, God completes the good work he begins at a Christian's Baptism within the Christian community. God completes this good work as the Christian lives with others in God's presence and responds with obedience through simplicity, prayer, and good works.

Classroom Activity

The students get a taste of the monastic life in this activity, which gives them the opportunity to pray the Liturgy of the Hours.

1. Before class, acquire a copy of the day's Morning Prayer from the Liturgy of Hours. You may find the prayer on the Internet at the Web site of either Universalis or Liturgy of the Hours Apostolate. If you prefer, you can locate the Morning Prayer in *Christian Prayer: The Liturgy of the Hours* (New York: Catholic Book Publishing, 1999). Make enough copies for everyone.

2. At the beginning of class, distribute the copies of the Morning Prayer, one to each student, and provide the following instruction in these or similar words:

❖ The spirituality of the Benedictine Order is to live each day in the presence of God. Monks seek God's face in their rhythm of communal work and prayer. Today we will say the Morning Prayer aloud from the Liturgy of the Hours, the prayer of the Church. Monks gather throughout the day to "sanctify the day" through this prayer.

3. For that part of the Morning Prayer when the psalms are recited, divide the class in half, and ask them to alternate their readings—first the group on the left, then the group on the right. (Less instruction will be needed if you preside; however, you may assign the role of presider to a student. You may also assign the role of reader to a student.)

4. After the class has prayed, and based on their reading of the selection, ask them the following questions:

❖ Why do you think someone would devote his or her life to such communal prayer and work?
❖ Would you be able to adopt such a life?
❖ Do you think it is important for the Church to have people devoted to such a life?

5. For student review, distribute copies of handout 12, one to each student, at a time of your choosing.

Homework Extension

Assign the following homework activity in these or similar words:

❖ If there is a monastery in your area, join the members for prayer one day. Also, arrange for a time to interview a Benedictine sister or monk, if possible. Ask her or him to describe the order's typical day and the members' spiritual practices.
❖ On the Internet, search for the Night Prayer from the Liturgy of the Hours. Pray the Night Prayer at the end of the day. Write a brief journal entry on what it was like to end your day with such a prayer.

A Father's Wisdom

A Guide for Living in a Community

Please provide complete answers to the following questions. You may need to record your answers on a separate sheet of paper.

Review Questions

1. In the prologue to *The Rule of St. Benedict,* what image does Saint Benedict use to describe each monk's relationship to God and to the religious superior?

2. What does Benedict say about the relationship between faith and good works?

3. What does Benedict say is the state of a human being's soul before that person accepts Christ?

4. When Benedict talks about opening a school to serve God, what does he say about the lifestyle the members of the community will follow?

5. How long should those who embrace this lifestyle plan to remain in a Benedictine monastery?

In-Depth Questions

1. Look carefully at the imagery used in the many Scripture passages woven into the text. List several of the references to the five senses you find. What might this imagery communicate about Benedict's vision of the communal life?

2. *The Rule of St. Benedict* has been admired for its balance and common sense. Find four examples in which Benedict seeks a balanced way of living the Christian vocation. How might these be helpful to you today?

3. What is the value of belonging to a small Christian community that shares a common vision and charism?

4. Most religious orders and congregations began as reform movements within the Church. What need for reform in the Church might have motivated Benedict to found a new religious order?

5. Read the Acts of the Apostles 4:32–37 and compare it with the picture of communal life Benedict presents in his *Rule.* How does this image compare with the hospitality that Benedictines are known for?

Saint Boniface: Missionary to the Germans

Summary of the Sources: "Letter Advising Saint Boniface on How to Convert the Heathens" and "Report to Pope Zacharias on the Foundation of Fulda Abbey"

Both the letter from Bishop Daniel to Saint Boniface and Boniface's own report to Pope Zachary on the founding of Fulda Abbey provide a window to the Church's missionary activity in the early eighth century. Bishop Daniel wrote as Boniface's friend, advising him to first listen to what the Germanic peoples had to say about their gods and then to guide them with clear arguments to see the supremacy of the Christian way. Boniface's letter to Pope Zachary reveals a certain humility and pragmatism, particularly as he dealt with corruption within the Church. Despite difficulties, Boniface spoke confidently of the good work he had accomplished, especially noting the establishment of the Benedictine monastery at Fulda.

Classroom Activity

Students learn about the different approaches to missionary activity as they compare the approach of Boniface to that of the contemporary Maryknoll missionaries.

1. Read aloud to the class the following passage from *Christianity Rediscovered,* by Vincent J. Donovan, who writes about his experience as a missionary in Africa:

> Paul's work resulted in the establishment of churches. We instead found missions. A permanent mission necessarily carries with it the atmosphere of foreignness, of colonialism. The word "mission" should really mean something in action, in motion, in movement, as it did for St. Paul. Mission compound, on the other hand, implies that the movement has come to a standstill. In the latter case, it is no longer a centrifugal force reach-ing out forever, as far as it can. It becomes instead centripetal, attracting everything to itself. Instead of symbolizing movement towards another thing (in this case, church) it becomes itself the end of the line. . . . The word "missionary" is really a misnomer in this context. The command to go out and preach the gospel has become subtly trans-formed into "Stay here, take care of what you have. Let others come to you." (P. 101)

2. After the reading, ask the class to compare Donovan's view with the ideas presented by Bishop Daniel and Boniface, using the following questions:

❖ Based on these readings, do you think that evangelization (spreading the Good News) is about setting up missions and telling the Good News to those who come to you? Or is evangelization a matter of being sent by the Christian community to find and recognize the Good News among the people you serve?

❖ How would each approach affect the people's cultures?

❖ If you were to go to a faraway land to do missionary work, what approach would you take?

❖ How do you think your chosen approach might work here at school?

3. For student review, distribute copies of handout 13, one to each student, at a time of your choosing.

Homework Extension

Assign the following homework activity in these or similar words:

❖ Go to a Catholic missionary organization's Web site. The Web site for the Maryknoll mission movement is a good one. Search for and read the organization's mission statement. Reflect on the meaning of the mission, and then write your answers to these questions: What is my personal mission for sharing the Good News at this time in my life? How can I best carry out my mission?

Saint Boniface

Missionary to the Germans

Please provide complete answers to the following questions. You may need to record your answers on a separate sheet of paper.

Review Questions

1. In "Letter Advising Saint Boniface on How to Convert the Heathens," what does Bishop Daniel say he wants Saint Boniface to accomplish among the Germanic people?

2. What approach did he advise Boniface to take?

3. What ultimate reason did Bishop Daniel give for converting people to Christianity?

4. In "Report to Pope Zacharias on the Foundation of Fulda Abbey," what are some of the problems within the Church that Boniface communicates to Pope Zachary?

5. How were the Benedictine monks at Fulda different from other clergy Boniface encountered?

In-Depth Questions

1. How would you characterize the type of argument that Bishop Daniel used to advise Boniface on how to convert the Germanic people? What value and limitations do this type of argument have?

2. What is Bishop Daniel's view of the culture of the Germanic people? Is his view similar to or different from the view of any other historical figure in the Church that you have studied?

3. Based on descriptions provided by Bishop Daniel and Boniface, what were some of the characteristics of the Church in the eighth century? Were there any signs that reform was needed?

4. How would you describe the role of the Pope at that point in Church history?

Conflicts of Faith: Tensions Between the East and the West

Summary of the Source: *Encyclical Letter to the Archiepiscopal Sees of the East*

After the Roman pontiff challenged Patriarch Photius's authority as a prelate, Photius responded with an incendiary letter to the patriarchs of the Eastern Church about some beliefs and practices in the Western Church. In so doing, he undermined the Pope's authority.

The letter listed several areas of disagreement. The most important was over the Trinitarian formula of the creed of Nicaea. The Roman Church had added a statement to the creed that said the Spirit proceeded not only from the Father but also from the Son. The other major disputes concerned the Roman, or Western, Church's attitude that priests who married were unworthy and the Roman directive that only bishops could confer the sacrament of Confirmation. Because these disputes became highly politicized, a major schism between the Eastern and Western churches eventually occurred.

Classroom Activity

Students will understand the Nicene Creed better as they uncover its essential elements.

Materials Needed
- ☐ newsprint
- ☐ markers
- ☐ four copies of *The Catholic Faith Handbook (CFH)* or of *The Catechism of the Catholic Church*
- ☐ four copies of the Nicene Creed

1. Divide the class into four groups and give each group a piece of newsprint, markers, a copy of the *CFH* or of the *Catechism,* and a copy of the Nicene Creed.

2. Assign one of the four parts of the creed to each of the groups. Group 1 will have the statement of belief in God. Group 2 will have the statement of belief in Jesus Christ. Group 3 will have the statement of belief in the Holy Spirit. Group 4 will have the statement of belief in the Church.

3. Have the groups each write the opening words to their assigned part of the creed at the top of the newsprint.

4. Ask the students to discuss within their group what the group's assigned segment of the creed means. They may refer to the *CFH* or the *Catechism* if they do not fully understand their segment.

5. Each group should briefly explain what the words of its segment mean as best they can, and write that explanation in the middle section of the newsprint.

6. At the bottom of the newsprint, each group should briefly explain why its assigned segment of the creed is important to Christianity.

7. Finally, invite the groups to present their findings to the class.

8. For student review, distribute copies of handout 14, one to each student, at a time of your choosing.

Homework Extension

Assign the following homework activity in these or similar words:

❖ Read the Apostles' Creed. Then choose one of the four "We believe" statements to interpret. How would you explain that section to someone who had never heard of Christianity before?

❖ Make a chart or a drawing that shows some of the most important people, beliefs, and relationships that you believe are necessary to bring together different Christian denominations as one Church again.

Conflicts of Faith

Tensions Between the East and the West

Please provide complete answers to the following questions. You may need to record your answers on a separate sheet of paper.

Review Questions

1. What major difference of opinion between the Western Church and the Eastern Church does Photius cite in his encyclical letter?

2. What is the stated fear in Photius's letter of what may happen to the Church as a result of changing a traditional belief?

3. How does Photius react to the Western Church's belief that priests should not be allowed to marry?

4. Why does Photius think that priests should be able to confer the sacrament of Confirmation?

In-Depth Questions

1. How would you describe the tone of Photius's letter? How might this tone affect the Eastern Church? How might it affect the Roman Church?

2. The controversy over the "Filioque" became the source of the most serious division between the Eastern and Western churches. Do you think that a traditional teaching can be changed or added to? If your answer is yes, under what conditions can changes or additions be made?

3. The Eastern Church continued to allow priests to marry, while the Western Church forbade the practice. What are the advantages and disadvantages of allowing priests to marry?

4. On Holy Saturday, the pastor of a Roman Catholic parish can confer the sacrament of Confirmation for candidates and catechumens. What are the advantages and disadvantages of being able to confer that sacrament all year as the Eastern Church does?

Chapter 15

Pope Against King: The Battle Over Appointing Bishops

Summary of the Source: "Correspondence Regarding Lay Investiture"

The correspondence between Pope Gregory VII and Henry IV illustrates the degree of seriousness that the problem of lay investiture had reached. Many appointments of bishops had become little more than political appointments. Gregory, also known as Hildebrand, withheld the customary apostolic benediction of Henry IV because the emperor had ignored Gregory's edict forbidding lay investiture and had appointed his own bishops in several dioceses. Henry in turn addressed Hildebrand as a false monk, certainly not a pope, and decried Gregory's attempt to usurp the rightful authority of a king to appoint bishops. Gregory made clear that his edict was intended to be an important reform and that it was by his authority as successor of Peter that the appointment of bishops belongs to the Church and not to earthly rulers. A line was drawn in the sand between the authority of the Church and the authority of the state.

Classroom Activity

The point-counterpoint debate in this activity focuses on this question: Should there be a separation between church and state?

1. Divide the class into two teams that will debate an issue related to the separation of church and state. One group will take the pro position, the other will take the con position.

2. Each group will decide who in their group assumes the following roles:

- **group leader** to keep the group on task
- **note taker** to take notes for the scribe
- **scribe** to write down the group's argument in point-by-point fashion
- **presenter(s)** to present each point the group wants to make to the class
- **resource person(s)** to provide information and ideas

3. Each group should consider the issue of faith-based drug rehabilitation programs. The state, as well as some church organizations, wants to help those who are addicted to drugs. Should government funds be used to help such organizations?

4. Allow time for each group to shape its argument. Then have each group present its side of the argument to the class. After the presentation, serve as the moderator for a debate on the topic.

5. After allowing enough time for a robust debate, conclude the debate by asking the following questions:

❖ Which point made by the other side is most compelling?
❖ What would you say to someone about the issue if the topic should come up outside of class?

6. For student review, distribute copies of handout 15, one to each student, at a time of your choosing.

Homework Extension

Assign the following homework activity in these or similar words:

❖ Call or visit the director of a faith-based organization that might receive government funding. Examples of such organizations are Catholic Charities, the Salvation Army, or a homeless shelter. Ask the director's opinion about receiving state assistance. You might find out how government aid helps, or could help, the organization or how such aid might limit the organization's work. Write a report on your interview.

Pope Against King

The Battle Over Appointing Bishops

Please provide complete answers to the following questions. You may need to record your answers on a separate sheet of paper.

Review Questions

1. In "Correspondence Regarding Lay Investiture," what, according to Pope Gregory, has Henry IV done that requires sincere repentance?

2. What authority does Gregory claim that the Church has in the appointment of bishops? What are his reasons?

3. According to Gregory, what is Henry's obligation toward the Church as a member of the Church?

4. From where does Henry believe he derives his authority as king or emperor?

5. What negative effect on the empire does Henry say will be the result of Gregory's edict?

In-Depth Questions

1. The framers of the Constitution of the United States established the separation of church and state. However, they also said that we walk on dangerous ground when laws are made without acknowledging God. How do you think belief in God should influence laws that are made?

2. Both the king and the Pope were powerful men who were both convinced they were right. In your opinion, who was wrong and who was right? Explain.

3. The Church says that Catholicism should not be too closely associated with one political party because if it is, it can lose its prophetic voice. Why do you think this is the case?

4. Name three political issues the Church cares deeply about. How do you think the Church can affect these issues without crossing the line between the separation of church and state?

"We Adore Thee, Lord Jesus Christ": The Last Words of the Tiny Friar

Summary of the Source: "The Testament of Saint Francis"

This last testimony of Saint Francis of Assisi illuminates his deep asceticism and love of Jesus Christ. In words that might seem strange to the modern world, Francis reminisces about his experience of a direct calling from God to a life of simplicity and poverty. He places himself among the least important in society and regards himself a servant of the Church. This testament is Francis's vision of central charism of his order, the Franciscans, and the vision he wished the friars to follow through faithfulness to the rule that is the foundation of the order. In essence, the testament is a call to evangelical poverty and powerlessness, even if it appeared to the world that this band of brothers was composed of "idiots," to use Francis's own word. In a time when the clerical state had become more and more associated with honor, the friars provided a prophetic alternative.

Classroom Activity

This activity helps students examine their attachment to material goods.

   1. Relay the following scenario to the students:

❖ Imagine you are going on a journey. You are on your way to a place where you will not want for anything. In fact, everything you have ever wanted is there. However, the journey will be long and hard. On this journey, you are allowed to take only five things with you, other than the clothes you are wearing. The five items have no size limit. The only stipulation is that they must be things you own. What five items would you bring?

   2. After allowing time for the students to make their lists, address the students in these or similar words:

❖ Saint Francis had an ability to make a complex world seem simple. He frequently used the simple image of a journey to describe life. Christians believe that this present life is a journey to the next life and that the choices made in this life create a destiny to be fulfilled in the next. Now take a moment to study your list of five items.

❖ Of the items on your list, which is most important to you?

❖ Francis's vision for his order of friars was that they travel light through life. Do you think Francis would call you a light traveler?

❖ Francis wanted his friars to live simply. Based on your list, do you think others would describe you as leading a life of simplicity?

   3. To conclude, read Matthew 6:21 to the students. Then ask them to write a one-page reflection on the following questions:

❖ Of all your possessions, which would you be most upset about losing? Why?

❖ Is this treasure important enough to possess your heart? Why or why not?

   4. For student review, distribute copies of handout 16, one to each student, at a time of your choosing.

Homework Extension

Assign the following homework activity in these or similar words:

❖ Saint Francis is known for his love of nature. Take a walk and pay attention to the natural world. What do you hear, smell, see, taste, and touch? How do you notice the presence of God? Say a prayer to thank God for his Creation and write a one-page reflection about your walk.

"We Adore Thee, Lord Jesus Christ"

The Last Words of the Tiny Friar

Please provide complete answers to the following questions. You may need to record your answers on a separate sheet of paper.

Review Questions

1. What experience led Saint Francis to embrace poor people as Christ himself?

2. How does Francis describe his relationship with the institutional Church and the clergy?

3. Briefly describe the life that Francis envisioned for the friars.

4. Why does Francis instruct the friars never to seek any office in the Church?

5. What is the importance of the Divine Office for the friars?

In-Depth Questions

1. What elements of Francis's address to his fellow friars make it truly a last will and testament?

2. For Francis, participation in the celebration of the Eucharist was clearly of great importance. Why did it have such importance? What difference might it make for you?

3. Some people measure the worth of a person by the number of possessions she or he has acquired. Do you think this is harmful? Why?

4. One modern principle of Catholic social justice is often stated something like this: Christians believe that until all have their basic needs met, none have a right to more than they can use. Do you agree? Explain.

Gentle and Powerful: The First Woman Doctor of the Church

Summary of the Source: "Letters to Pope Gregory XI"

The two letters of Saint Catherine of Siena to Pope Gregory XI present a view of reality that defies the modern logic of the powerful. Armed with a profound conviction in Christ, Catherine candidly and forcefully challenged the Pope to return the Papacy to Rome from Avignon. She saw that political turmoil and instability seriously threatened the Church's unity. Catherine's spirituality and mysticism garnered respect from the Pope. Such respect allowed her to challenge the Pope to stand up as a "manly man" to the forces that threatened the Church.

Classroom Activity

The students look at their sources of fear and stress and discover how a personal relationship with Jesus can guide a person onto the right path.

1. Ask the students to each write down a list of their fears or things that cause them stress.

2. Ask two students to come to the board to list the students' fears as you ask for them. Invite the students, one at a time, to name some of their most common fears or causes of stress. You might find it necessary to participate to provide a more complete list.

3. Ask the students to choose as a class the top six fears or sources of stress that high school students face from the list on the board. Then ask the students to respond one at a time to the question: What difference does a personal relationship with Jesus Christ make in responding to those fears and causes of stress?

4. Explain how Catherine's personal relationship with Jesus gave her the courage to speak frankly with the Pope.

5. Ask the students to reflect on the following statement:

❖ The language of fear is not the voice of God. God is love and perfect love casts out all fear. The language of God is always the language of love and courage.

After a few moments of silence, lead the students in the following prayer:

❖ Lord our God, you gave Saint Catherine of Siena the courage to speak the truth. Give us your Holy Spirit. May your Holy Spirit help us in times of fear and stress to always do what is right, speak what is true, and do what is loving. We ask this through your Son, Jesus the Lord. Amen.

6. For student review, distribute copies of handout 17, one to each student, at a time of your choosing.

Homework Extension

Assign the following homework activity in these or similar words:

❖ Find a quiet place where you can write. With paper and a pen in front of you, turn out the lights. Light a candle and focus on the light in the darkness. Then prayerfully write a list of your greatest fears on the left side of the paper. Next, ask God for light as you write down how you think God wants you to respond to each fear. End by praying the Our Father.

Gentle and Powerful

The First Woman Doctor of the Church

Please provide complete answers to the following questions. You may need to record your answers on a separate sheet of paper.

Review Questions

1. In her letter to Pope Gregory XI, what reasons does Saint Catherine of Siena give for writing?

2. What reasons does Catherine give Gregory for returning the papacy to Rome?

3. What does Catherine communicate to Gregory about the role of obedience to Christ?

4. Why does Catherine exhort the Pope to be a "manly man"?

In-Depth Questions

1. Catherine devoted her life totally to Christ and became a mystic at a very young age. What difference, do you think, did this fact make in her challenge of the Pope?

2. Does anything that Catherine said appear to you to be insulting to the Pope? Would you be insulted if she wrote to you in that way? Explain.

3. Catherine was a person of tremendous integrity; she was a person of prayer and a servant of the poorest of the poor. What difference does personal integrity make at a time when it is important to confront evil and injustice?

4. An important theme of Catherine's letters to the Pope is that a Christian should be obedient to the will of Christ and that a person of faith should not fear. Carefully consider what Catherine said about obedience and fear. What might have convinced Gregory to believe that Catherine was truly speaking for Christ and calling the Pope to do God's will and overcome his fears?

Revival of Prayer: A Springtime for Spirituality

Summary of the Source:
The Imitation of Christ

Though they may not choose the same words as Thomas á Kempis, most Christians would agree with his intent: always seek truth and seek to love God first. A good conscience and true peace belongs to the person who seeks truth. Such a person can patiently withstand adversity because the way of God is the way of truth. Thomas also wrote that the world calls us to a variety of loves and friendships, but no love or friendship is greater than a commitment to Jesus Christ. However, the notion that a choice must be made between our loyalties to God and our loyalties to other people may seem disconnected. Yet, if we consider that Thomas was speaking during an age of widespread corruption in both the Church and the state, his intent becomes clear: God must come first in all our relationships.

Classroom Activity

Students examine the reading from *The Imitation of Christ* and translate the key points of the reading into contemporary concepts.

Materials Needed
☐ newsprint
☐ markers

1. Divide the class into groups of four or five students. Ask the groups to each appoint a reader, a scribe, and one or more group presenters.

2. Provide the groups with the following instructions:

❖ For centuries *The Imitation of Christ* has been considered a handbook for Christian living. This exercise will give you an opportunity to revise "The Seventh Chapter: Loving Jesus Above All Things" from that book by putting it into contemporary language that young people today can better understand.

❖ Turn the newsprint sideways and make three columns. At the top of the three columns, the scribes should write these phrases: "ideas we like," "ideas we don't understand," and "ideas we would like to add."

❖ Now, as a group, carefully go through "The Seventh Chapter: Loving Jesus Above All Things," with your group's scribe filling in columns 1 and 2 as you read.

❖ After you have completed that task, look at what your group has written. Then, in column 3, have your scribe add ideas that your group members feel would help make this chapter more understandable to young people today.

❖ When you have finished, your group's presenters should share with the class what your group believes is most important for teens to hear today about loving Jesus above all things.

3. Conclude by asking the students to make a list of three ways they can personally put the words of Thomas á Kempis into practice.

4. For student review, distribute copies of handout 18, one to each student, at a time of your choosing.

Homework Extension

Assign the following homework activity in these or similar words:

❖ Choose a contemporary song—religious or secular—that you think speaks really well to what friendship is all about. Listen to the song, imagining as you listen that Jesus Christ is the friend the song is about. Be prepared to bring this song for the class to hear.

Revival of Prayer

A Springtime for Spirituality

Please provide complete answers to the following questions. You may need to record your answers on a separate sheet of paper.

Review Questions

1. What difference does it make, according to Thomas á Kempis, to live truthfully and according to your conscience?

2. What does Thomas say about the way God considers deeds and motives?

3. What kind of relationship with Jesus does Thomas advise?

4. According to Thomas, what is the nature of the relationships the world offers?

In-Depth Questions

1. Thomas's view of the world was simple and easy to understand: You should do good and avoid evil. On a scale of 1 to 10, how well do you rate when you must choose between right and wrong? Explain.

2. After reading what Thomas wrote about conscience, how would you explain the meaning of **conscience**? Do you believe your own conscience is a good guide for judging what is right or wrong? Explain.

3. Describe the qualities of true friendship. Do you believe Jesus can be your best friend? Explain.

4. Make a list of the things or the people you are loyal to (examples: friends, family, school, God). List these loyalties from highest to lowest priority and briefly explain why they are important. What place do you feel Jesus Christ should occupy among all of these different loyalties?

The Revolutionary Monk: The Protestant Reformation Begins

Summary of the Source: "Writings from Martin Luther"

Martin Luther wrote with fiery boldness as he addressed the Christian nobility of Germany. His letter demonstrates the conviction with which he proceeded. Although perceived to be a fool, Luther feels his foolishness is the wisdom of God.

In his commentary on Romans, he conveys the heart of his theology: Salvation is a free gift and is a work that God does within us. Salvation cannot be earned by doing good works. At the same time, Luther did not discount the value of good works. In fact, his understanding was that wherever true faith exists, good works inexorably follow.

Classroom Activity

In this activity, students take weighty issues of the day and prioritize them through a consensus process.

1. Explain to the students that this exercise is about reaching consensus and that they will have to use their best listening skills. Invite a student to come to the blackboard. Ask the other students to take out a piece of paper and a pencil or pen.

2. Ask the class to brainstorm the most important issues humanity faces (abortion, war, poverty, the environment, and so on). As the students name the issues, the volunteer should write them on the board.

3. Instruct the students to list all the items from the board on their paper, ranking the items by their order of importance.

4. Have the students then find a partner. The partners should work together to identify the top three issues and then rank these three issues in order of importance.

5. Then ask the pairs to each tell the class which issue they have chosen as their number-one issue.

6. Groups that have ranked the same issue as most important should then form a group and write a statement that conveys their reasons for choosing that issue.

7. Have each group (from the smallest to the largest) read its statement to the class and explain the ranking of the issue.

8. Allow time for discussion and ask the following questions:

❖ Now that you have heard the rationale of other groups, is anyone inclined to change which issue is ranked most important?

❖ Is it possible that several issues are equally important?

❖ How did you decide between two seemingly equal issues?

9. For student review, distribute copies of handout 19, one to each student, at a time of your choosing.

Homework Extension

Assign the following homework activity in these or similar words:

❖ In a journal, a notebook, or on a piece of loose-leaf paper, write the story of a time when you had a good idea rejected by others. Provide detail about how you felt then and how you would deal with such a situation today. Do you think Martin Luther had similar feelings? Do you think his actions made matters worse for him?

The Protestant Reformation Begins

Please provide complete answers to the following questions. You may need to record your answers on a separate sheet of paper.

Review Questions

1. In his writings, why does Martin Luther say that the audience for whom his letter is intended might consider him presumptuous?

2. How does Luther define faith?

3. What illusion of faith does Luther criticize?

4. What is the relationship of faith to good works, according to Luther?

In-Depth Questions

1. Many people say, as Martin Luther did, that we live in troubling times. If you were writing a handbook for communicating during difficult times, what advice would you give about communicating with people with whom one disagrees?

2. Luther was excommunicated from the Church. That is, he was declared to have removed himself from the community of salvation. In your opinion what type of offense, if any, warrants excommunication?

3. Luther said that faith in God is being certain of his love and care. This confidence gives a peace and happiness that cannot be found elsewhere. How does your faith compare with this description?

"What Is Necessary Is a Different Approach": The Catholic Reformation

Summary of the Source:
The Way of Perfection

Saint Teresa of Ávila grieved over the division in the Church and the loss of Christians to the Protestant Reformation. Seeing so many uncommitted Catholic Christians led her to reason in *The Way of Perfection* that if God did not have many friends, then the friends God had should be good ones! She was determined to be a good friend to God and to have those in her monasteries be good friends to God. In reforming her Carmelite order, Teresa proposed a new approach, one that differed from the Church's previous efforts to overcome the influence of the Protestant reformers. Instead, she proposed fortifying the faith from within through prayer. Teresa called upon her Discalced Carmelites to withdraw from the world, to live completely on the charity of others, and to make prayer for the servants of God in the Church their vocation.

Classroom Activity

This activity helps the students discover two ways of overcoming evil—by force and by persuasion.

Materials Needed
☐ newsprint or poster board
☐ various magazines with pictures
☐ glue sticks

1. Divide students into groups of four or five and distribute the materials among the groups.

2. Write "By Force vs. By Influence" on the board. Ask the groups to each write "By Force vs. By Influence" across the top of their poster board. They should then draw a line down the center of the poster board, with one half falling under "By Force" and the other half under "By Influence."

3. Instruct the students to think about situations they have encountered in school. On one side of the poster board, ask them to briefly write words that describe at least three situations that external, forceful means were used to effect student behavior. On the other side, they are to describe the way student behavior was affected through influence or from within. Such situations may include inspiring presentations given during an assembly. Challenge them to be creative and specific.

4. After the groups have completed their posters, engage the class in a discussion about whether force or influence might have the greatest immediate effect, either positive or negative. Then ask the students which method would have the greatest long-term effect.

5. Conclude by asking the following questions:

❖ Would you describe Teresa's methods as force or influence?
❖ Why did she choose this method?
❖ If or when is it appropriate to use force?
❖ Is there something wrong in society that you could help overcome through influence? How so?

6. For student review, distribute copies of handout 20, one to each student, at a time of your choosing.

Homework Extension

Assign the following homework activity in these or similar words:

❖ In *The Way of Perfection,* Saint Teresa says that there is nothing that those who love one another cannot handle peaceably. Write a one-page reflection describing a conflict in your experience where love of one another helped bring a resolution and a conflict where love was forgotten.

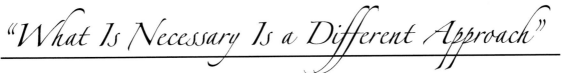

"What Is Necessary Is a Different Approach"

The Catholic Reformation

Please provide complete answers to the following questions. You may need to record your answers on a separate sheet of paper.

Review Questions

1. In *The Way of Perfection*, what reason does Saint Teresa of Ávila give for founding her small group of Discalced Carmelites?

2. What did Teresa believe happens to those who leave the Church?

3. Is there any indication that Teresa saw problems within the Church itself?

4. What comparison did Teresa use to describe the manner of living that her Discalced Carmelites had chosen?

In-Depth Questions

1. How did Teresa distinguish between the success of external force and the success of the interior strength of faith? Where have you experienced this type of discussion today?

2. Because the number of Christians was large, why did Teresa comment that God did not have many friends? Do you think that God still has only a few friends? How would you describe a friend of God?

3. Teresa said that she prayed for the intentions of her benefactors, even when they asked for wealth and money. But she also wrote that she did not think God heard her prayerful requests for the material success of her benefactors. How do you think God answers self-centered prayers?

4. Teresa was deeply concerned about division within the Church. Do you think that the Church will always be divided over differing opinions? How might people with various opinions find that they enjoy greater unity than they do division?

"Nor Should They Be in Any Way Enslaved": Europeans Encounter the West

Summary of the Sources: *Inter Caetera* and *Sublimis Dei*

Popes Alexander VI and Paul III represent two sharply contrasting approaches to the peoples of foreign lands. In his writings to King Ferdinand and Queen Isabella of Spain, Pope Alexander VI advocated the use of force to win converts to Christianity. As he indicated in *Inter Caetera*, Alexander VI equated evangelization with the expansion of the Christian empire. The devastating consequences of this approach were the actions of European explorers, who ruthlessly and forcefully conquered native peoples and showed little regard for their human dignity and rights. In contrast, Pope Paul III recognized that all human beings are endowed with the same human capacities and basic rights. He condemned slavery and demanded respect for the human dignity and freedom of all people.

Classroom Activity

By comparing previous methods of evangelization with the Church's present-day practices, the students learn how to proclaim the Gospel message while respecting other cultures.

1. View the documentary film *Columbus Didn't Discover Us: Perspectives on the Quincentennial* (1992, 24 minutes, not rated).

2. After viewing the film, lead the students in a discussion by asking the following questions:

❖ What negative results of colonialism did you learn about from the video?

❖ Did you learn anything about the Church's role?
❖ What positive aspects of indigenous culture did you learn about?
❖ How should modern missionaries proceed among different cultures, such as Native Americans?

3. Address the students in these or similar words:

❖ Pope John Paul II has promoted a new evangelization. This new evangelization proclaims the Gospel message to all peoples while respecting the culture of others. This approach recognizes the good within a culture and tries to bring that culture to greater perfection by preaching the person of Jesus Christ. With this understanding of evangelization, how would you have brought the Gospel to the native peoples if you were with Columbus? Write a one-page reflection that demonstrates your methods.

4. For student review, distribute copies of handout 21, one to each student, at a time of your choosing.

Homework Extension

Assign the following homework activity in these or similar words:

❖ Read Christopher Columbus's diary entry from October 13, 1492. This and other excerpts from Columbus's diary may be found at Internet sites like the Internet Medieval Sourcebook from the Fordham University Center for Medieval Studies.
❖ With this description of the native peoples as Columbus encountered them, create a Christian symbol that might speak to the people. You may use any materials you wish.

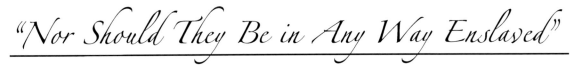
"Nor Should They Be in Any Way Enslaved"

Europeans Encounter the West

Please provide complete answers to the following questions. You may need to record your answers on a separate sheet of paper.

Review Questions

1. What method of bringing Christianity to indigenous peoples of foreign lands did Pope Alexander VI advocate?

2. Considering Alexander VI's comments about the kingdom of Granada, what role did land play in his view of the spread of Christianity?

3. How did Alexander VI understand the use of force in accomplishing his goals?

4. What did Pope Paul III say are the most important characteristics of all human beings?

5. Describe Paul III's position on slavery.

In-Depth Questions

1. Make a list of the things that Alexander VI said bring proper glory to the Church. Do you think that these items bring proper glory to God? Explain.

2. Based on the words of Alexander VI, how do you think he understood these words from the first Creation story of Genesis: "Fill the earth and subdue it" (Genesis 1:28, NRSV)? Explain.

3. What, according to Paul III, are the most important human capacities? Do you agree? Would you add to or change anything that he says?

4. Do you believe that people are created to receive truth? What sometimes gets in the way of some people's capacity to understand the truth?

People of Esteem: The Work of Missionaries in China

Summary of the Source: "Letter to Francesco Pasio, SJ, Vice-Provincial of China and Japan"

In his letter, Mateo Ricci explains the divine, practical, and natural ways that people in China received Christianity. He believed that Christianity could be embraced by a large number of Chinese. One reason for his optimism was the value the Chinese placed on intellectual activity. He thought it was possible to convey the reasonable truths of Christianity to the most educated and powerful people. Also, the ability to use books to share the faith had a tremendous effect because it allowed people to read about Christianity in a complete way and made it easier for Chinese converts to share the faith with others in their country. Ricci found that the Chinese are naturally intellectual and pious. They were eager to learn the sciences, which can be a step toward understanding faith. Despite the Chinese people's worship of idols, Ricci found that the Chinese had followed natural law throughout their history.

Classroom Activity

In this activity, students imagine missionaries approaching the leaders in modern countries, and they make parallels with Mateo Ricci's letter.

1. Divide the class into several small groups of three or four students.

2. Ask the groups to each assume the identity of a Catholic missionary team whose assignment is to convert powerful people in a foreign country to Catholicism, as Mateo Ricci did in China. Ask the groups to each answer the following questions as part of their scenario:

❖ Who are the most powerful, or elite, people you would visit?

❖ Would you be welcomed or turned away?

❖ Would you have enemies? Who might they be?

❖ What do the powerful people prize? Can you use what they value as a tool for sharing the Good News? How?

❖ What kind of skills or means would you employ to communicate the Catholic faith to those you are evangelizing?

❖ Can you share information or experiences with the elite that would eventually lead them to the Catholic faith?

❖ Where do you see points of agreement between your message and the concerns or practices of those you evangelize?

3. Ask the class to share the results of the planning done in their small groups. Encourage the students to share any insights they received from this exercise. Conclude by noting that a successful missionary observes who people are, assesses their strengths, speaks to them in a way that makes sense, meets their intellectual needs, and uses successful means of communicating the message.

4. For student review, distribute copies of handout 22, one to each student, at a time of your choosing.

Homework Extension

Assign the following homework activity in these or similar words:

❖ Write a two- or three-paragraph reflection on these questions: In what ways does missionary work resemble advertising? What distinguishes missionary work from advertising?

People of Esteem

The Work of Missionaries in China

Please provide complete answers to the following questions. You may need to record your answers on a separate sheet of paper.

Review Questions

1. In his letter to Francesco Pasio, SJ, what reasons does Matteo Ricci cite for a feeling of security in China?

2. Ricci mentioned two characteristics held in great esteem in China. To what characteristics did he refer?

3. Why did Ricci think it would be easy to convince the kingdom's leader?

4. Why did Ricci think books were important in his work?

5. Why did Ricci say the Chinese were inclined toward piety?

In-Depth Questions

1. Ricci said that he first earned the esteem of, or the respect of, the Chinese people. What must someone do to earn your esteem or respect?

2. Ricci expressed the vision of the Jesuit order. His and their vision is to convert the world's leaders to the Gospel in the hopes of bringing the Gospel to everyone. However, many believe the Gospel is best received not by the elite but by society's poorest members. Are these ideas opposed to each other? Explain.

3. Ricci mentioned the role of scientific discovery in his mission work with the Chinese. Why do you think science can be an important part of preaching the Gospel?

4. Apparently books were important in Ricci's missionary work. If you were to think of this country as missionary territory, what would be as important to us as books were to the Chinese? Explain.

Money, Workers, and Fairness: Catholic Social Teaching Begins

Summary of the Source:
Rerum Novarum

Rerum Novarum begins with a rationale for the Church's issuing of this document on a secular matter—the rights of workers. *Rerum Novarum*'s author, Leo XIII, viewed this workers' rights document in the same light as previous Church documents that refuted erroneous teachings or beliefs. He viewed the abuse of workers as such an error. *Rerum Novarum,* which speaks against Communism, proclaims the people's rights to own property, decries the divisiveness of class envy, and states the rights of families to live without government intrusion. It also objects to extreme capitalism as it articulates the rights of workers to organize and warns against a pursuit of material goods that neglects spiritual matters. Overall, *Rerum Novarum* seeks to bring unity to humanity and to bring humanity to salvation. To this end, this encyclical speaks against the ways labor divides the human family and the way temporal pursuits distract from the eternal.

Classroom Activity

This activity introduces the students to the ways they can use their own work and labor to bring glory to God.

1. Review the primary source with the students, emphasizing its groundbreaking stance on the rights of the worker.

2. Ask the students to take out a sheet of paper and a pen or pencil. At the top of the paper, they are to write "Dream Job."

3. Address the students in these or similar words:

❖ What is your dream job? You can write anything. There are no limits other than the fact that it must be a real job in today's work environment.
❖ Now answer the following five questions about your dream job:

- What is this best thing about your dream job?
- How would you describe the income level of your dream job? Low pay, middle pay, high pay, or extremely high pay?
- Do you think your dream job will help your relationship with God? Why or why not?
- How could your dream job help others?
- Based on your answers to the previous questions about your dream job, what is most important to you?

4. Review again with the students the main points from *Rerum Novarum* and reiterate the Church's vision for work and labor. Then ask the students to write a one-page reflection that answers the following questions:

- In my classwork, extracurricular work, household chores, or current job, how can I be sure that God is honored and praised in my work?
- As I move forward in life toward a career, what will I need to remember from *Rerum Novarum* to help me work as God is asking me to work?

5. For student review, distribute copies of handout 23, one to each student, at a time of your choosing.

Homework Extension

Assign the following homework activity in these or similar words:

❖ Research child labor practices. Most young people in your country have a wonderful opportunity to pursue a fulfilling career. But in many parts of the world, young children are forced to work in demeaning or dangerous jobs. Search the Internet for information and then use that information to write a two-page report on child labor. Your report should include reasons why companies use child labor and why families allow their children to work in such conditions. Name any specific companies your research uncovers.
❖ Create a collage that demonstrates child labor practices.

Money, Workers, and Fairness

Catholic Social Teaching Begins

Please provide complete answers to the following questions. You may need to record your answers on a separate sheet of paper.

Review Questions

1. Why did Pope Leo XIII think it was important for the Church to issue a document on labor?

2. How did the socialists try to remedy the problem of poor people's envying those who were rich?

3. Why did Leo XIII reject the socialists' remedy?

4. Why did Leo XIII say that worker associations should be able to organize?

5. Toward what is the working person to be urged?

In-Depth Questions

1. A large section of *Rerum Novarum* is devoted to the problem of envy between classes. Why was there a need to address this problem?

2. The socialists had a remedy for resolving class envy. How did they propose to solve the problem of the gap between rich people and poor people?

3. In most cases, the United States government does not interfere with the price of products or services. What are the dangers in this system?

4. *Rerum Novarum* reminds its readers that the ultimate goal of each individual is to reach eternal life with Jesus Christ. How can work help one achieve that goal? How can work distract one from that goal?

The Vicar of Christ:
The First Vatican Council Defines Papal Authority

Summary of the Source: *Pastor Æternus*

In *Pastor Æternus* the First Vatican Council provides a clear statement justifying and defining the doctrine of papal infallibility. This statement was a response to significant cultural changes in the world that were considered potential threats to the institution of the Church. This document clearly strengthens the authority of the Papacy and draws a clear line of distinction between believers of the Church and those outside of the Catholic Church. *Pastor Æternus* roots the doctrine of papal infallibility in the historical councils of the Church and ultimately in the establishment of Peter as the first pope.

Classroom Activity

This activity helps the students see the scriptural roots of the doctrine of papal infallibility.

1. Begin by asking the students for their initial reactions to *Pastor Æternus*.

2. Next, have the students, as a class, define the Papacy by sharing phrases, titles, and traits they associate with the Papacy. Record their answers on the board.

3. Divide the class into groups of three or four and ask the groups to read the following passages from the Scriptures:

- Matthew 16:17–19
- John 21:15–17

4. Ask the groups to each answer the following questions based on the list on the board and on their reading of the Scripture passages:

❖ What in the Scripture readings explains the establishment of Peter as the first pope?

❖ What in the Scripture readings explains the foundation of the doctrine of papal infallibility?

❖ Where do you see the spirit of the Scripture readings present in the primary source reading?

5. Bring the groups back together and have them share their answers to the questions. Allow time for discussion and note any questions they have about the topic. Encourage the students to spend time in prayer and reflection on their questions.

6. For student review, distribute copies of handout 24, one to each student, at a time of your choosing.

Homework Extension

Assign the following homework activity in these or similar words:

❖ A great deal of confusion surrounds the first dogma a pope defined through papal infallibility—the doctrine of the Immaculate Conception. Research what the Immaculate Conception is and what the Church teaching is concerning it. Write a one-page essay defining and explaining the significance of the Immaculate Conception.

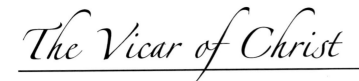
The Vicar of Christ

The First Vatican Council Defines Papal Authority

Please provide complete answers to the following questions. You may need to record your answers on a separate sheet of paper.

Review Questions

1. Whom does *Pastor Æternus* describe as the leader of the Apostles?

2. What terms does *Pastor Æternus* use to describe the power of the pope's jurisdiction over the Church?

3. How did the Council of Florence define the pope?

4. How does *Pastor Æternus* describe or define the term *ex cathedra*?

In-Depth Questions

1. Why, do you think, was the word *anathema* used in the document?

2. Some say that *Pastor Æternus* gave too much authority to the pope. Others say that Jesus intended for Peter and his successors to have such authority so they could maintain the unity of the faithful. Why do you think it might be important for the pope to have supreme teaching authority?

3. *Pastor Æternus* places a lot of importance on the pope's being a direct successor of Peter. Why, do you think, is this important?

4. In your own words, define the term *ex cathedra*.

Year in the Life: An Account of Life in the Spanish Colonies

Summary of the Source: "Report on the Mission of San Carlos de Monterey"

The "Report on the Mission of San Carlos de Monterey" provides a glimpse into life at the Spanish missions in California. It contains details about the founding of the mission and the subsequent years. The work, the spiritual life, and the number of people affected by the mission are mentioned in the report. But most interesting is the description of communal life shared by the laypeople residing within the mission. Many questions have been raised in recent years over Fr. Junípero Serra's methods of evangelization. However, the description of the Christian community shared by those in the mission is indeed reminiscent of the community described in the Acts of the Apostles.

Classroom Activity

This activity helps the students name the major events in their school community over the past twelve months and see God's presence in those events.

1. Ask the students to review the reading from Fr. Junípero Serra by naming some of the significant events cited in his report.

2. Then tell the students that as a class, they are to review the significant events in the life of the school. Invite a student to record on the board the students' answers to the question: What are the most significant, whether happy or sad, events in the life of the school community over the past twelve months? Allow plenty of time for the students to name several events. After a considerable list has been generated, ask the students to name the five most important.

3. Read Psalm 139:7–10 (below) to the class:

Where can I go from your spirit? Or where can I flee from your presence? If I ascend to heaven, you are there; if I make my bed in Sheol, you are there. If I take the wings of the morning and settle at the farthest limits of the sea, even there your hand shall lead me, and your right hand shall hold me fast. (NRSV)

4. Now address the students in these or similar words, following up with a discussion based on the reflection question:

❖ This psalm says that God's presence is everywhere. He is in the light and the dark. We have taken a look at our community's most significant events from the past twelve months. Some brought happiness, others sadness. But this psalm says that God's presence was in all of these events. Try to think like the writer of the psalm thought. How can you see God's presence in each of these events?

5. Ask the students to silently say a prayer of thanks for God's presence in the school. Allow time for the silent prayer and then offer a prayer of thanksgiving for God's activity in the lives of the students.

6. For student review, distribute copies of handout 25, one to each student, at a time of your choosing.

Homework Extension

Assign the following homework activity in these or similar words:

❖ The "Report on the Mission of San Carlos de Monterey" illustrates someone's looking back at the activities in a community and seeing God's activity among the people. Look back over the past twelve months in your own life. Write a one-page reflection that answers these questions: What are the five most significant events that have happened to you? In these events, how have you seen God's presence?

Year in the Life

An Account of Life in the Spanish Colonies

Please provide complete answers to the following questions. You may need to record your answers on a separate sheet of paper.

Review Questions

1. When was the mission of San Carlos de Monterey founded?

2. How did Fray Junípero Serra celebrate the founding of the mission?

3. Why did Serra consider 1783 such an outstanding year in the mission?

4. How many new Christians lived in the mission in 1783?

In-Depth Questions

1. The early account of the mission's establishment tells of Serra's activity in a new world as a missionary. If you could choose anywhere in the world to be a missionary, where would you go? Why there? What kind of work would you want to do?

2. The establishment of the mission was the founding of a community of people that worked, prayed, and ate together. If you were living in such a community, what would you like best about it? What would be the most difficult part of living in such a community?

3. Serra's report indicates that over 5,000 people had been affected by the mission's work for Jesus Christ. In a single day, how many different people do you have contact with? Do you think you positively affect these people? Provide an example to explain your answer.

Concern for Souls:
A Bishop's Anxiety over the Faith of Slaves in Mississippi

Summary of the Source: "A Letter to the Society for the Propagation of the Faith"

Bishop William Henry Elder's 1858 report on the diocese of Natchez is both touching and disturbing because it shows the virtues and the errors of the Church's presence in the nineteenth-century American South. Elder bemoaned the neglect of the slaves because of a shortage of priests. He expressed a sincere concern for slaves' souls; yet his report concomitantly reveals his own misunderstanding of the logic of oppression. Unable to perceive the injustices perpetuated by slavery, he concluded that the slaves themselves are morally weak, fickle, ignorant, and naturally dependent upon others. Such comments strike the twenty-first-century ear as being blatantly racist. However, Elder also describes the slaves as immortal beings in God's image. This reading demonstrates a confused morality that might help illumine modern confusion as well.

Classroom Activity

This activity helps students discover issues in today's society that the message of the Gospel counters.

1. Have the students share what they find to be positive and negative in the reading. It might be useful to first present a brief overview of the role and importance of slavery in the South at the time Bishop William Henry Elder wrote the letter.

2. Next ask the students to discuss why they think the letter was written. In particular, have them identify what motivated Elder to write the letter and what he hoped to accomplish.

3. Explain that Elder's letter, though saturated with negative stereotypes of the time, stood opposite to popular sentiment in the South and called for action based on the Gospel message that challenged the norms of nineteenth-century Southern society.

4. Have the students identify beliefs or trends in today's society that counter the beliefs of Christianity. List their ideas on the board. Their answers might include violence and consumerism.

5. Ask the students to each select one of the topics listed on the board. They should research whether the topic has been addressed by the bishops. If it has, write a letter thanking the bishops for addressing the issue. If it has not been addressed, draft a letter asking the U.S. Conference of Catholic Bishops for specific help addressing the issue. These letters should include the following items:

- an introduction to the topic
- why it is important to confront this issue
- Scripture quotes explaining why we must challenge this issue
- who is affected by this issue
- specific actions the bishops can take
- what you are willing to do to confront the issue

6. Have a few students share their letters with the class.

7. For student review, distribute copies of handout 26, one to each student, at a time of your choosing.

Homework Extension

Assign the following homework activity in these or similar words:

❖ Watch the movie *The Mission* (1986, 126 minutes, rated PG) and identify scenes that remind you of Bishop Elder's letter. Also, note the arguments made by the characters in support of and in defiance of slavery. Write a one-page report on your findings.

❖ Search for Church documents that address the issue of slavery. Possible starting points are the *Catechism of the Catholic Church* and the Vatican Web site. Select one major document and identify common points between the document and Elder's letter.

Concern for Souls

A Bishop's Anxiety over the Faith of Slaves in Mississippi

Please provide complete answers to the following questions. You may need to record your answers on a separate sheet of paper.

Review Questions

1. At the time of Bishop William Henry Elder's letter, what proportion of the population of Mississippi was Catholic? What percentage of the state's people were slaves?

2. What was Elder's chief anxiety?

3. Where did the slaves go to school and to church, if and when those things were available to them? Why?

4. How did Elder describe the character of the Negro slaves?

In-Depth Questions

1. Based on his letter, what do you think motivated Elder to express such great concern for the slaves?

2. If it is true that many slaves seemed engrossed with satisfying their bodily desires, what do you think accounted for this? Would you agree with Elder that these things are instinctual?

3. In his letter, did Elder criticize the system of slavery? Why do you think he kept himself within certain boundaries of discussion?

4. Do you believe that there are instances today when people fail to see the full consequences of their words or actions because they accept a system without question? If so, explain your answer.

5. As you read the letter, how did you feel? Did you experience any hurt or anger?

More Than a Tabloid: The Power of *The Catholic Worker*

Summary of the Source:
The Long Loneliness

In *The Long Loneliness,* Dorothy Day presents an overview of the mission of *The Catholic Worker,* the tabloid she published. She also reveals the forces that drove its development over the years. Early in the reading, she introduces the reader to those who are poor and explains why Christ holds a special connection to poor people through his incarnated experiences. Dorothy goes on to address the conditions that *The Catholic Worker* was striving to counter, and she responds to charges that *The Catholic Worker* was a communist collaborator.

Classroom Activity

This activity helps your students identify the poor people in their midst, just as Dorothy Day did. You will need an assortment of newspapers. If you have access to the Internet for your students, you can have them use online versions of newspapers.

1. Begin by having the students share what they believe makes someone poor. Encourage them to think beyond monetary issues. List the students' responses on the board. You may choose to direct them to the fourth paragraph in the selected reading.

2. Divide the class into groups of two to four students. Each group is to compile a collection of ten to fifteen stories, advertisements, and pictures from the newspapers and magazines that reveal forms of poverty. Have them consult the list on the board.

3. Invite the groups to each share with the whole class their group's top three or four stories, advertisements, or pictures. After all the groups have shared, initiate a class discussion about what is being done to alleviate the instances of poverty they have identified.

Homework Extension

Assign the following homework activity in these or similar words:

❖ Obtain a recent copy of *The Catholic Worker.* Read and report on the issues presented in it. In your report, identify the organizations and the individuals who are working on the same issues in your local area.

❖ Research the life of Peter Maurin, the cofounder of *The Catholic Worker,* and answer this question: How did Maurin help shape the development of the Catholic Worker movement? You might consider watching the movie *Entertaining Angels: The Dorothy Day Story* (1996, 112 minutes, rated PG-13).

More Than a Tabloid:

The Power of *The Catholic Worker*

Please provide complete answers to the following questions. You may need to record your answers on a separate sheet of paper.

Review Questions

1. In *The Long Loneliness,* whom did Dorothy Day identify as the audience for *The Catholic Worker?*

2. What goals did the Catholic Worker Movement share with socialist or communist groups that led to the movement's being accused of collaborating with such groups?

3. Identify at least four groups that Day said *The Catholic Worker* had strived to help.

4. What reason does Day give for *The Catholic Worker's* coverage of international issues?

In-Depth Questions

1. Explain how the Incarnation of Christ shaped Dorothy Day's understanding of what it means to be of service to those who are poor.

2. How does the Catholic Worker Movement express the dignity of all God's children and respect for God's Creation? Provide specific examples from the selected reading.

3. Day describes her actions as controversial and unpopular. Why, do you believe, was the *The Catholic Worker* considered controversial or unpopular? What stands out about *The Catholic Worker* that runs counter to popular American ideals?

4. Read the Beatitudes (see Matthew 5:1–12), noting as many examples from the reading as possible that you believe respond to specific beatitudes.

Traitor to the State, Herald of the Gospel

Summary of the Source: "Letters from a Nazi Prison"

From behind the walls of a Nazi prison in Austria, Franz Jägerstätter wrote this letter to his wife explaining his decision to defy the Nazis. His decision to resist led to his execution in the waning years of World War II. Jägerstätter's letter expresses the challenge of being a Christian and making tough decisions based on one's faith, particularly when those decisions affect people he or she loves. The letter reveals the turmoil Jägerstätter experienced in standing up to the Nazis and sacrificing his life with his wife and children for the sake of his beliefs.

Classroom Activity

This activity explores the role of faith in marriage and family. In particular, it stresses that of all our relationships, our relationship with God must come first.

1. Begin a discussion about the reading by asking the following questions in these or similar words:

❖ Do you agree with Jägerstätter's decision to take a stand against the Nazis, running the risk of leaving his family without a father?

❖ How do you think his decision made his wife feel?

❖ When his children were older, do you think they understood his decision?

❖ What other options, do you think, did Jägerstätter have?

2. Divide your class into five groups. Assign each group one of the following readings:

- Romans 12:1–2,9–18 (selected reading for the conferral of the sacrament of Marriage)
- Hebrews 13:1–6 (selected reading for the conferral of the sacrament of Marriage)
- John 15:12–16 (selected reading for the conferral of the sacrament of Marriage)

- 2 Timothy 2:8–13; 3:10–12 (selected reading for the Common of Martyrs)
- John 17:11–19 (selected reading for the Common of Martyrs)

3. Ask the groups to review the writing of Jägerstätter and compare it with their assigned Scripture reading. Have the students, in their groups, answer the following questions with examples:

- How do the actions of Jägerstätter reflect what is being asked for people to do in the reading?
- How does the reading offer comfort to Jägerstätter's wife and children?
- Does the reading say anything that might be counter to Jägerstätter's actions?

4. Ask the groups to each share their assigned reading or prayers with the class and present their answers to the questions.

5. Allow time for class discussion around the responses to the questions or any other questions the students might have.

6. For student review, distribute copies of handout 28, one to each student, at a time of your choosing.

Homework Extension

Assign the following homework activity in these or similar words:

❖ Research the life and death of Saint Maximillian Kolbe and compare his actions to those of Franz Jägerstätter. What are a few aspects common in the lives and the deaths of both men?

❖ Select one of the martyrs of the Catholic Tradition and write a one-page summary of her or his life that includes why that person was martyred. A few possibilities are Saint Stephen, Saint Joan of Arc, Jean Donovan, Saint Perpetua, Oscar Romero, and Saint Agnes of Rome.

Traitor to the State, Herald of the Gospel

Please provide complete answers to the following questions. You may need to record your answers on a separate sheet of paper.

Review Questions

1. In the third paragraph of the reading from "Letters from a Nazi Prison," what does Franz Jägerstätter identify as the role of a Christian?

2. What are the three reasons Jägerstätter gave his wife to explain his actions?

3. Why would Jägerstätter not trade his cell for a palace?

4. What does Jägerstätter believe the Our Father will be for his children?

In-Depth Questions

1. Do you admire Jägerstätter for standing up for his beliefs, or do you think he was selfish for not staying with his family? Explain.

2. Why did Jägerstätter believe that taking the military oath would be a form of lying? Explain whether you believe this would be an acceptable lie in light of the consequences.

3. If you were placed in the same situation as that of Jägerstätter, what would you do? Why?

4. Have you ever been in a situation where standing by your convictions brought about discomforting consequences? If so, describe the situation.

Reading the Signs of the Times: The Church in the Modern World

Summary of the Source:
Gaudium et Spes

After centuries of looking inward, the Church positioned itself in the very midst of the world rather than remaining an institution standing apart from the world. In fact, *Gaudium et Spes* links the future of the Church to the future of the human race in the midst of uncertain circumstances. Its famous opening line claims that the joys and anxieties of the human race are the same joys and anxieties of the Church. This is a Church not only of the hierarchy but also of the laity—a Church called to serve, to witness to the truth, and to rescue, not to sit in judgment. Ultimately, the Church is to read the signs of the times—that is, to *listen*—so that it can speak credibly and intelligibly to a new generation, particularly to young people, poor people, and those who are afflicted.

Classroom Activity

Modern-day martyr Archbishop Oscar Romero may be best known for saying that all are members of the Church. In this activity, students reflect on both the strengths and the needs of young people today. They will then write a letter to the bishop of their diocese, expressing their ideas and concerns.

1. During the class before the day of this activity, explain to the students what they will be doing during the activity. Invite a student to compose a prayer to begin the next class. Also, ask two students who are good at writing to write the letter that will be sent to the bishop.

2. On the day of the activity, remind the students that the purpose of the activity is to find common agreement about both the strengths and the needs of young people and to express those concerns to the bishop in a letter. Begin the class with the prayer composed by the student.

3. Invite one student to list students' comments from steps 4 and 5 on the board and another student to record those same comments on a sheet of paper.

4. Invite the students to brainstorm with one another about their greatest strengths and the assets they bring to the Christian community, while the two students selected record their thoughts.

5. Then repeat the process as the students describe their greatest needs as young Christians.

6. Ask the students to prioritize both lists from most important to least important. Then ask them to create summary statements that include the greatest strengths and needs of youth today.

7. Ask the two students you recruited the day before to write a letter based on their summary statements to the bishop. Mail the letter to the bishop and include a cover letter explaining the activity and its purpose.

8. For student review, distribute copies of handout 29, one to each student, at a time of your choosing.

Homework Extension

Assign the following homework activity in these or similar words:

❖ Create a drawing, poem, collage, or even a short piece of music or lyrics that expresses the notion that "the Church is all of you."

Reading the Signs of the Times

The Church in the Modern World

Please provide complete answers to the following questions. You may need to record your answers on a separate sheet of paper.

Review Questions

1. How does *Gaudium et Spes* describe the Church?

2. According to this document, the Church is to read the **signs of the times.** What are some of those signs of the times the document mentions?

3. What has been the effect of modern life and technology on religion, according to this document?

4. Why does the document express particular concern for the young people of today?

In-Depth Questions

1. The Church, over many centuries before the Second Vatican Council, had often described itself as a spiritual reality set apart from the world. However, in *Gaudium et Spes,* the Church says that its destiny is truly linked to the destiny of the entire human race. Can both be true? Explain.

2. Considering the vision of the Church offered in *Gaudium et Spes,* can you think of a situation in today's world that needs the Church's presence? What could the Church do to benefit this situation?

3. *Gaudium et Spes* speaks of technological advancements long before the dawn of the Internet. Read the **signs of the times.** How, do you think, can the Internet benefit human dignity? How does it threaten human dignity?

4. Why is it vitally important today that the Church be able to speak to the young people of the world in a way that is intelligible and meaningful to them? How have you seen today's Church communicate more effectively with young people?

The Light of the World: The Church as the Sacrament of Salvation

Summary of the Source:
Lumen Gentium

Lumen Gentium calls all members of the Church to become a priestly people, the light of Christ to a world in need. The tone of *Lumen Gentium* is that of urgency. The tremendous needs of the modern world cry out for a visible response from the Church. This response should affirm the freedom and dignity of all people and bear witness to Christ. This document is also a prophetic statement about the role of the laity to transform the structures of society by using their own unique gifts, cultures, and technologies to bring Christ to the ends of the earth in ways not yet imagined.

Classroom Activity

In this activity the students explore the fact that the Church is the Body of Christ, of which we are all members. We all have gifts that are vital to a healthy Church. (Have a candle available for this activity.)

1. Tell the students they will be focusing on the gifts of each person in the class. Consider playing soft instrumental music through step 3.

2. Ask the students to write down the first name of each person in the class. If necessary, you could supply a class list to each student.

3. Ask the students to think of a quality they admire or a gift they see in each person and write each person's quality or gift next to his or her name.

4. When all have finished, light a candle and dim the lights. Pass the candle to the first student in the front row and ask the students to name a quality they see in someone in the class they want to imitate. Tell them to name only the quality and not the person. Have the student holding the candle pass it to the student on his or her left. Repeat the process and continue until all have participated.

5. Next, read 1 Corinthians 12:4–11 to the class. After your reading, turn the lights up and invite volunteers to share what they felt or learned from this experience.

6. Conclude by emphasizing the importance of these gifts to the Church. You might also compile the qualities and gifts from the students' lists to give to each student the next day.

7. For student review, distribute copies of handout 30, one to each student, at a time of your choosing.

Homework Extension

Assign the following homework activity in these or similar words:

❖ Prayerfully read 1 Corinthians 12:27–31. In a journal or on a piece of paper that you will keep, write about the gifts you can bring to the Church and how you think you will use those gifts in the future.

The Light of the World

The Church as the Sacrament of Salvation

Please provide complete answers to the following questions. You may need to record your answers on a separate sheet of paper.

Review Questions

1. What does *Lumen Gentium* suggest from the very beginning that the role of the laity in the modern Church will be?

2. How does *Lumen Gentium* describe the makeup of the early Christian community?

3. What is the mission of this **messianic people**?

4. What is the role of the sacraments in the life of God's priestly people on earth?

In-Depth Questions

1. *Lumen Gentium* calls the Church to be a sacrament or visible sign to the world. It says that laypeople have a unique role in the Church because they are in closer contact to the rest of the world than the clergy are. Name three specific ways that laypeople can bring the light of Christ to the world in ways that are different from those of a priest.

2. About forty years have passed since the close of the Second Vatican Council. Do you think that the increased role of the laity in the evangelization of the world as described in this document has been fulfilled? Why or why not?

3. What do you think the Church needs from you to fulfill its mission of being the light of Christ?

4. How is the role of the modern family described? How would you describe the role of the family today within the Church? Describe your vision of a family that lives as a light of Christ.

Chronological Listing of Chapters

The numbers in the first column represent the year or range of years relevant to each chapter. The second column is the title of the chapter. The third column is the page number for the material in the student text. The fourth column is the page number for the related material in the leader's guide.

Years(s)	Chapter Title	Page	Page
54–90	Expanding the Church: The Gentiles and the Mosaic Law	27	16
70–90	The Descent of Holy Spirit: The Church Is Revealed	21	14
80–120	From Movement to Institution: Practices and Guidelines for the Early Church	33	18
112	Executions and Torture: The Treatment of Christians During Roman Persecution	38	20
202–203	The Blood of the Martyrs: A Witness to Love for Jesus	43	22
311–313	New Freedom: The Roman Empire Offers Toleration to Christians	50	24
413–426	Two Cities: The Earthly and the Heavenly	56	26
451	True God Became True Human: Statements on Who Jesus Is	62	28
530–560	A Father's Wisdom: A Guide for Living in a Community	76	32
723–751	Saint Boniface: Missionary to the Germans	81	34
731	Missionary Pope: Saint Gregory the Great Brings the Light of Christ to England	69	30
867	Conflicts of Faith: The Tensions Between the East and the West	88	36
1075	Pope Against King: The Battle Over Appointing Bishops	95	38
1226	"We Adore Thee, Lord Jesus Christ": The Last Words of the Tiny Friar	102	40
1376–1377	Gentle and Powerful: The First Woman Doctor of the Church	107	42
1425	Revival of Prayer: A Springtime for Spirituality	112	44
1493	"Nor Should They Be in Any Way Enslaved": Europeans Encounter the West	127	50
1520–1522	The Revolutionary Monk: The Protestant Reformation Begins	117	46
c. 1565	"What Is Necessary Is a Different Approach": The Catholic Reformation	122	48
1609	People of Esteem: The Work of Missionaries in China	133	52
1784	Year in the Life: An Account of Life in the Spanish Colonies	150	58
1858	Concern for Souls: A Bishop's Anxiety Over the Faith of Slaves in Mississippi	156	60
1862	The Ship of Salvation: The Church as an Institution	17	12
1870	The Vicar of Christ: The First Vatican Council Defines Papal Authority	144	56
1891	Money, Workers, and Fairness: Catholic Social Teaching Begins	138	54
1943	Traitor to the State, Herald of the Gospel	169	64
1952	More Than a Tabloid: The Power of *The Catholic Worker*	162	62
1964	The Light of the World: The Church as the Sacrament of Salvation	179	68
1965	Reading the Signs of the Times: The Church in the Modern World	174	66
1977	Initiation into a Community: The Body of Christ as a Model of the Church	11	10

Topical Index

The first page number relates to the student text, and the second page number relates to the leader's guide.

Bishops, Writings from
Concern for Souls: A Bishop's Anxiety Over the Faith of Slaves in Mississippi 156 *60*
Conflicts of Faith: The Tensions Between the East and the West 88 *36*
Saint Boniface: Missionary to the Germans 81 *34*
Two Cities: The Earthly and the Heavenly 56 *26*

Christian Living, Guides to
A Father's Wisdom: A Guide for Living in a Community 76 *32*
From Movement to Institution: Practices and Guidelines for the Early Church 33 *8*
Revival of Prayer: A Springtime for Spirituality 112 *44*
Two Cities: The Earthly and the Heavenly 56 *26*
"We Adore Thee, Lord Jesus Christ": The Last Words of the Tiny Friar 102 *40*
"What Is Necessary Is a Different Approach": The Catholic Reformation 122 *48*

Church, Models of the
Initiation into a Community: The Body of Christ as a Model of the Church 11 *10*
Ship of Salvation: The Church as an Institution, The 17 *12*

Church, Nature of the
Descent of the Holy Spirit: The Church Is Revealed, The 21 *14*
Expanding the Church: The Gentiles and the Mosaic Law 27 *16*
Initiation into a Community: The Body of Christ as a Model of the Church 11 *10*
Light of the World: The Church as the Sacrament of Salvation, The 179 *68*
Reading the Signs of the Times: The Church in the Modern World 174 *66*
Ship of Salvation: The Church as an Institution, The 17 *12*
Two Cities: The Earthly and the Heavenly 56 *26*

Church, Origins of the
Descent of the Holy Spirit: The Church Is Revealed, The 21 *14*
Expanding the Church: The Gentiles and the Mosaic Law 27 *16*
From Movement to Institution: Practices and Guidelines for the Early Church 33 *18*

Church, Theology of the
Light of the World: The Church as the Sacrament of Salvation, The 144 *68*
Reading the Signs of the Times: The Church in the Modern World 174 *66*
Vicar of Christ: The First Vatican Council Defines Papal Authority, The 144 *56*

Church, Women in the
Blood of the Martyrs: A Witness to Love for Jesus, The 43 *22*
Gentle and Powerful: The First Woman Doctor of the Church 107 *42*
More Than a Tabloid: The Power of *The Catholic Worker* 162 *62*
"What Is Necessary Is a Different Approach": The Catholic Reformation 122 *48*

Dogmatic Statements
Light of the World: The Church as the Sacrament of Salvation, The 179 *68*
True God Became True Human: Statements on Who Jesus Is 62 *28*
Vicar of Christ: The First Vatican Council Defines Papal Authority, The 144 *56*

Ecumenical Councils
Expanding the Church: The Gentiles and the Mosaic Law 27 *16*
Light of the World: The Church as the Sacrament of Salvation, The 179 *68*
Reading the Signs of the Times: The Church in the Modern World 174 *66*
True God Became True Human: Statements on Who Jesus Is 62 *28*
Vicar of Christ: The First Vatican Council Defines Papal Authority, The 144 *56*

Evangelization
(*See* Missionary Activity)

Jesus Christ, Nature of
True God Became True Human: Statements
on Who Jesus Is   62   *28*

Missionary Activity
Concern for Souls: A Bishop's Anxiety Over
the Faith of Slaves in Mississippi
156   *60*
Missionary Pope: Saint Gregory the Great
Brings the Light of Christ to England
69   *30*
"Nor Should They Be in Any Way Enslaved":
Europeans Encounter the West   127   *50*
People of Esteem: The Work of Missionaries
in China   133   *52*
Saint Boniface: Missionary to the Germans
81   *34*
Year in the Life: An Account of Life in the
Spanish Colonies   150   *58*

North America
Concern for Souls: A Bishop's Anxiety Over
the Faith of Slaves in Mississippi
156   *60*
More Than a Tabloid: The Power of
The Catholic Worker   162   *62*
Year in the Life: An Account of Life in the
Spanish Colonies   150   *58*

Persecution
Blood of the Martyrs: A Witness to Love for
Jesus, The   43   *22*
Executions and Torture: The Treatment
of Christians During Roman Persecution
38   *20*
New Freedom: The Roman Empire Offers
Toleration to Christians   50   *24*
Traitor to the State, Herald of the Gospel
169   *64*

Pope, Actions of
Gentle and Powerful: The First Woman
Doctor of the Church   107   *42*
Missionary Pope: Saint Gregory the Great
Brings the Light of Christ to England
69   *30*

Pope, Relationships with Secular Authorities
"Nor Should They Be in Any Way Enslaved":
Europeans Encounter the West   127   *50*
Pope Against King: The Battle Over
Appointing Bishops   95   *38*

Pope, Statements from
Money, Workers, and Fairness: Catholic
Social Teaching Begins   138   *54*
"Nor Should They Be in Any Way Enslaved":
Europeans Encounter the West   127   *50*
Vicar of Christ: The First Vatican Council
Defines Papal Authority, The   144   *56*

Pope, Theology of the
Gentle and Powerful: The First Woman
Doctor of the Church   107   *42*
Vicar of Christ: The First Vatican Council
Defines Papal Authority, The   144   *56*

Reformations, Protestant and Catholic
Revolutionary Monk: The Protestant
Reformation Begins, The   117   *46*
"What Is Necessary Is a Different Approach":
The Catholic Reformation   122   *48*

Sacraments, Practice of
From Movement to Institution: Practices and
Guidelines for the Early Church   33   *18*

Scriptural Readings
Descent of the Holy Spirit: The Church Is
Revealed, The   21   *14*
Expanding the Church: The Gentiles and the
Mosaic Law   27   *16*

Social Justice
Money, Workers, and Fairness: Catholic
Social Teaching Begins   138   *54*
More Than a Tabloid: The Power of
The Catholic Worker   162   *62*
"Nor Should They Be in Any Way Enslaved":
Europeans Encounter the West   127   *50*